Autographed!
The Pathway to Becoming a Masterpiece

Darrell Dobbelmann
Dove Publications

Autographed

© 2016 by Dove Publications. All Rights Reserved.

Dove Publications is the publishing arm of Dove International and is designed to serve its' Statement of Purpose which exists to create Christian Leaders who will change the Nations.

Published by Dove Publications
P.O. Box 97
Glenwood, MN. 56334

Cover Design by Sarah Schuetty

Printed in the United States of America

ISBN: 978-0-9977264-0-4

Library of Congress Cataloging

To my dad Theodore Dobbelmann; to my first Bosses, Ken Olson and Bob Strom; to my first (and always) Pastor, David Jones; to my NCU Professors, Orel Krans & Don Meyer; to my first YWAM Leader, Oren Paris; to my first YWAM Partner, Clark Barnard; to my friend and President of Key Ministries, Steve Holte; and to all those bold men and women who taught me by their example that life is not a nest to inhabit, nor is it a veil to hide behind, but it is God's great opportunity for me to get out in front and bravely lead others to Their Dreams!

Table of Contents

Preface

Introduction

Dedication

Chapter 1-A Feat of Engineering Genius
Chapter 2-Bonafide Union Labor
Chapter 3-The Day It All Changed
Chapter 4-The Cloverleaf Twins
Chapter 5-Monkees or Morons
Chapter 6-The Miracle Wig
Chapter 7-Green Bugs and Politics
Chapter 8-The Vision in My Living Room
Chapter 9-Converting the Den of Iniquity
Chapter 10-Brown Hair and A Bandanna
Chapter 11- Most Prominent Homosexual
Chapter 12-The Voice of God
Chapter 13-Ashes and Broken Buttons
Chapter 14-Operation Love Lift
Chapter 15-Wayne Snyder
Chapter 16-The Ambassadors
Chapter 17-Guns and a Long Awaited-Baby
Chapter 18-The Dove Arrives
Chapter 19-The Greatest Joy
Chapter 20-The Oasis
Chapter 21-Celebrating
Chapter 22-The Finished Painting

Preface

A dictionary defines "Autograph" in two ways:
1) "A valuable manuscript, masterpiece, or work of art created solely by the hand of its author or creator"
2) "A person's handwritten signature"

"Autographed" will perform a marriage between these two definitions. This book enjoins each of us <u>to be</u> the unique and wonderful "Autographs" that we are intended to be!

COME WITH ME

My wife and I saw a beautiful sunset recently by the shores of Lake Minnewaska. This is the lake in the lovely Minnesota town where we reside called Glenwood. My wife and I have seen many sunsets over the lake, but last night was unique! The sun was setting underneath the cloud cover and it illuminated them with a blaze of colors from the underside! It was literally like God wrote with a great paintbrush all across the sky and even over our heads in huge beautiful swaths of reds, oranges, and yellows. All accented by the blue of the sky and the white and grays of the clouds. We thought of the wonderful Creator-Father who gives His children *"all things richly to enjoy".*

The most wonderful and the most promising thing He gives us are our own lives! How much He wants us to enjoy those lives to the max! Instead, so many of us hinder His Handiwork and stay His Creative Hand with our own ways. Ways that are often marred by erroneous desires. The outcome ends up being a marred autograph! I pray that as you read, you and I will take a journey together. Our time will be fun and most of all it will empower you to live, love, and interact in a more thrilling way with others. My sincere desire is that this will be a time of discovery of who you are; of what you were meant to be, and a time of yielding to the Brushstrokes of the One who paints the sky!

This book contains the Brushstrokes of the One Who is Perfect! I am the canvas. These are my stories.

I have been in hundreds of different speaking and ministry venues in my life. So often, someone who had attended a previous seminar will make a request of me and say, "Darrell, Tell them about such and such a story". You know the one where..." I am honored that so many have loved my stories. I know that they love them because the creative Hand of God so powerfully purchased them.

My story telling ability started with my mom. She was very dramatic. Her eyes would flash brightly; her face would grimace or smile. She would make up stories that always conveyed some truth about being a good person, being obedient, or loving others. I still love telling made-up stories or other people's stories, but these will be my own real life stories with a message! I wish I could even tell you these stories in person. Maybe someday.

I've been challenged so many times to put these stories in writing! I'm sixty six and I'm visiting three nations again in the next three months. Many of the places I go are rift with Christian persecution and danger. The older I get, the more I realize how vulnerable I am!

Even while I'm writing this I'm sitting in a hotel in Bhubaneswar, India. I've just returned from doing a big Pastors' Seminar in a village about 8 hours from here where some Hindu radicals began to riot. They had two pastors evicted from the town for baptizing someone in a nearby river. They were looking for more Christians and I was eating in the hotel restaurant. They were coming in the front door and I went out the back. I missed them by seconds. I stayed locked in my friends' room as the radicals were trying to get the Hotel Manager to show them the hotel registry. Luckily, he did not and when things died down, I returned to my room, went to sleep, and then snuck out at 4 AM.

Then I went to another town to another seminar and I was called into the Police Station for questioning. I walked by the jail door with its thick bars and the thought passed my mind, "I sure hope I don't end up in there!" I told the chief that I was there to honor the people, and the culture, and to respect his authority and I assured him that if he had any problem with what I was doing, to just come talk to me and I'll change it. We laughed and talked as his assistants checked me out on their computers. He finally gave me some tea; we laughed together, and he sent me on my way. We had over 200 church leaders and Pastors at the meeting in that town and we strategized how to win the neighborhoods and plant new churches. It is such a privilege to be working in the great country of India during the time that God has chosen for hundreds of millions to be saved! Then, yesterday, the Indian Intelligence called and asked questions about where I was and where I'll be going. I've always felt God's protection, but since I know I'm mortal, my vulnerability seems to stare me down more each year.

So I'm finally taking the advice of those who say, "you've gotta write a book, and you've gotta tell those stories. People will learn so much from them".

Here's my goals for "Autographed":
1. **Honor!** To honor the Autographer!
2. **Freedom!** Life is the greatest journey for all of us! "Autographed" is written so that you can receive new Freedoms as you read it.
3. **Laughter!** Enjoy the stories!
4. **Legacy!** "Autographed" is about making the most of yours!

Every life is amazing; yours is amazing! Come walk with me! The Bible says that true fellowship is to have a "**participative sharing**" in each others life. Our lives are blended with some wonderful experiences. Each life and experience has its own wonderful flavor. "Variety is the spice of life". Take my hand and let's walk together with my Friend. Just the three of us! Here's a great adventure and I want you to be in on it!

GRATEFUL FOR THE REAL THING!

A Movie Star may just sign a piece of paper...but because of who it is, even that piece of paper becomes valuable. But I am intrigued most by those famous Artists, Musicians, and Sculptures who have used their best time, tools, and talent to produce a treasure and THEN put an autograph on it! Now the signature authenticates a creation that is their own creation!- A TRUE AUTOGRAPH!

When a Famous person puts his/her Autograph on something like a painting, a musical score, or even a baseball, that object has great value, but when a similar but fake object has a forged signature on it, it is by nature, fraudulent! A counterfeit!

When a counterfeit is discovered, it becomes a matter of shame for the perpetrator and the object is of very little worth.

On the other hand, a very valuable Treasure can exist for ages and <u>suddenly</u> be discovered and determined to be authentic. When this genuine "Autograph" has been discovered, it is renowned and even celebrated!

Break out the Champaign!

Could you be one of the world's hidden treasures?

Here's a story about someone who discovered me. I grew up in a dysfunctional home where my step- father would tell me I would never amount to anything. When he threw me out of the house at 17 years of age, I quit school and was forced to seek early employment. I got a job at a Plastics manufacturing plant. I was surprised to see the President and Vice-president notice that I had mechanical abilities and even leadership giftings. They began to mentor me and advance me. It was a wonderful feeling to be "discovered"! After all, I had been told I was a loser for years!

Something in all of us wants to be discovered, mentored, and advanced by a great Master and then live out the success of what has been invested in us!

Here's the 1st question: Can we autograph ourselves? I certainly could not! I was hurt, disappointed, fearful, and damaged! Oh, certainly I did my best to cover it up, but my underlying nature was damaged and discouraged. <u>The</u>

nature of a true masterpiece is that it can never be self-created!

Here's the 2nd question: Can others autograph us? They might try; especially if we ask them. They may do it as a favor. Friends are always ready to bestow encouragement, but they can never bestow Identity!

So we must be careful seeking "brush strokes" from friends on our personal "Canvases". Asking someone to sign our yearbook is one thing; signing our life canvas is quite another. We can end up cheating ourselves, our Identity, and our Destiny by seeking anyone but "The Author" to put the brush strokes on our Canvas. Invariably, others will refine us, but they must never define us! Unfortunately we all have a need for this thing called Approval, and it gets us into trouble sometimes! We seek input that ends up not helping us, but marring us! We end up hurt, bitter, discouraged, feeling used, or even worse...we may even feel like some forger has meddled with our very identity!

To be fair, not everyone we might seek for approval has evil intents. Some may even be hungry for another's "brushstrokes" themselves! I'm sure you've seen two well meaning but needy people seek each other's input and both end up getting hurt! Once that happens, we try to scrub away the brushstrokes they made on our lives, but those strokes seem so indelible sometimes!

Many times we simply want another's affirmation. We didn't even seek their input, but instead of affirmation we get criticism or they just don't notice.

We are social creatures. This world can be a painful place sometimes. Is there any answer?

> *Invariably, others will refine us, but they must never define us!*

The Bible says, "*Owe no man anything except to love them*". We don't owe them praise, we can't give them happiness, and we can't depend on them for ours!

Here's a 3rd question: How about Colleges? They can bestow a degree upon us! That should be a great boost to us discovering ourselves...right? Should that be our Autograph? We may take great pride in the "shingle" we hang on our wall, but in reality it is only (and at its best), just one of the "Brushstrokes" that can be used by the Master to develop our lives.

What about this 4th question: How about job positions and titles? That was certainly a boost to me! Yes, maybe this is the answer! My career became a very refreshing Oasis after the dry desert of my childhood. But as I accumulated wealth, I still found it impossible to forgive those who had wronged me; I was still miserable in my heart, and it was very difficult to build deeply meaningful relationships because I wanted to control everything. Did position and income finally autograph me? The answer to this question was unfortunately a big "NO"! Money, cars, respect, and even a home still did not Autograph my identity.

Ah, but then the Master Painter showed up! I remember when I met that Amazing Person. It happened when I was 23. It was the most profound meeting of my life! He turned His head toward me and looked me in the eyes from the cross He was dying on. He said, "Darrell, I did this for you". In that moment, I abandoned my search for human Autographs. Now, His Brush Strokes are completing me!

They are the only things that are completing me; and they are wonderful! Jesus said, *"Come unto me all you who labor and are heavy laden and you will find rest for your soul. Take my yoke upon you and learn from me for I am gentle and humble of heart, and you will find rest for your souls"* His Pen alone must autograph us! Only then can we be free from all the baggage that comes from seeking identity from other sources. All the other things will be used by His hand to refine us, but never to define us! Then thousands will be touched by you, and as your life touches them, they will be amazed by your Creator!

This is the only cure!

Our destiny is waiting, but our determination must be to seek it's completion from the Hand of the One who is the Master Creator of Destinies!

Millions seek short cuts and attempt to autograph themselves or seek others to do it, and by doing it, these individuals never discover their identity or value!

He waits for you to surrender so He may begin to write.

The destiny that you can posses was never created for any other human being. You are an ORIGINAL!

The great thing about surrendering to the Hand of God is that He autographs you first and completes you later! You are His Masterpiece right away! He's proud of you right off the bat! You're perfect from the start! You have identity before He even takes out His Paint Brush! How does He do this?

> *A Painter signs a work after he's sure it's perfect; God autographs you before the work has begun!*

Let's look at the definition of a "Signature" and maybe that will help us understand the wonder of this immense love. **A Signature signifies 4 things: 1)agreement, 2)approval, 3) payment, or 4)ownership.**

<u>**Christ has done all four with you!**</u>
    He agrees with and owns your life! How could He not agree with it! He made it! Ok, you most likely have done a lot of messing it up. He doesn't agree with all your activities and choices, but the sacrifice of Christ on the cross has created a harmony between God and you <u>despite what you have done</u>. *"He has made the two (former alienated individuals) one, by breaking down the wall of hostility that once existed between the two"* Ephesians 2:14. This is the truth! Do you believe it?
    He approves your life! He approves it! He defends it in justice before His Father. He stands against other's & the Devils' accusations of you, and instead represents your worth and perfection because those things are "imputed" to you at your Spiritual Birth! In spite of all your errors, you are indeed His Son or Daughter as soon as you receive Him! Then the Bible says "we were justified by His resurrection". Next Easter, think about your life and yourself being <u>created</u> and then <u>defended</u> by the world's greatest Creator/Lawyer-Jesus the Christ! *"Who is He that condemeth, it is Christ who justifieth..."* Romans 8.

He paid for you! He made personal payment for you while you were helpless. *"We were not purchased with cheap things like silver and gold, but by the precious Blood of Jesus Christ".* 1 Peter 1:18. The highest payment possible was paid for you; the Blood of the Creator. Why? Because you are worth it! I've heard some Evangelists thunder with words like, "We were worthless creatures". No! Why would Christ pay for something that was worthless? Unworthy, yes; but never worthless.

He owns your life! *"To all who received Him- to all who believe on His name He gave the right to become Sons of God".*

The only outstanding question then is...Have you received Him? If not, God will honor a simple personal prayer of yours right now to give you a **New Birth** into His family. STOP, BOW, PRAY, and SURRENDER right now; then the angels will rejoice! Now you have finally found the Master Painter! His signature is on your Life's Canvas right now! You are already signed and about to become an Original Masterpiece of your Father King!

Introduction

BRUSHSTROKES

The continual Brushstrokes of Christ in our lives are crucial to our identity. Even if we shrink away from past failures and pains, then those things will occupy a throne that will dictate our activities and attitudes every day! Let's joyfully come to Christ now as we remember that He is not surprised by our wrongs, our pains, or our shames. Christ is not subservient to any of the mistakes you make....or that you've made! He's Lord! Lord of your past, your birth, your sin, your holiness, and your future. Christ means to de-throne the controlling fears of those memories and fill your memories with clarity and grace. He desires to remove those fears and pains from the thrones they have deceptively occupied, and use them as a new story of His greatness in your life! Be assured; Jesus wants freedom to govern all you are and all you do *"It is for your freedom that He set you free"* – Galatians 5

So the words of this song must be the <u>cry of our hearts</u>:

> *"Come write Your Name in this clay! Come put your name on this picture!"*
> -Julie Meyer

No more "forged names" written by the deceiving pens of religiosity, image, fear, or self. No more hiding my heart, closing my doors, and lowering my spiritual shades.

Come Lord Jesus! Autograph me. Own every experience, every fear, and every shamed place of my past. Fill me with confidence! Let life make sense! Make me an ambassador of your compassion.

THE BIRTHPLACE OF OUR LIFE STORIES

Our lives are filled with pains and scars, as well as joys & achievements. <u>These not only become our greatest stories</u>, but they also become our great victories as well! <u>God autographs our past in this way:</u> He builds our trust in Him until we can face even the most painful or difficult things like memories and entrenched habits. One by one He enables us to face things with His reasoning rather than our own. We discover priceless eternal truths as we go through them.

Then we owe to our loved ones the transmission of these testimonies! *"We are Living Letters known and read among men, so now with unveiled faces we reflect the Lord's Glory to others as we ourselves are being continually transformed into His Likeness"* 2 Corinthians 3:3 & 18

These are precious and personal life lessons. Far too valuable to be in a vault of silence! What story is God incubating in your life right now? Here's the key: Always endeavor to keep a biblical attitude and then the story will turn into a life lesson!

The stories herein are of Christ writing His personal autograph over my pains, my past, my parts, and all the portions and all the pieces of my life! His freedom has empowered me to no longer repeat them in habitual bondage; to never cower under them in fear, but to have them be a "readable" and redeemed display of His Power in a world that so often doesn't make sense! May all of our stories become hope to others that we are not helpless victims of sickness, pain, damaged relationships, and adversity. Most of those contained in these pages are my own. In a world that "just doesn't make sense" could these wounds be doorways of opportunity for others to meet Christ face to face?

"The sufferings of this age are not worthy to be compared to the glory which shall be revealed in you! For God is working in you a far more exceeding weight of glory"

WHERE DOES HOPE COME FROM?

Naturally from God and His grace! ... but there is a formula! It says in Romans 5:3 that it comes from having the right attitude during hard times. Out of that comes a life style of perseverance, and from that grows the wonderful quality of hope!

The extra benefit of hope, it goes on to say, is it makes us so we are not ashamed! Isn't shame a horrible thing? The Bible has the only formula to be free of it. What a wonderful formula for confidence in life!

<u>Here's the Divine formula of Romans 5:</u> **Hardship plus a Biblical Attitude= Perseverance= Personalized hope = A Confident Life**

A GIFT OF EVER-INCREASING FREEDOM

I pray this book be a gift <u>to you!</u> Maybe the best gift you've ever had! That you may undergo an "Autographing Transformation" as you read it! I hope that your life, and its freedom, and destiny will become contagious to your kids and all those around you. I want Christ's Brushstrokes on your life to be a gift of inspiration to them that will outlast your life on earth in their memories.

You say, "Darrell, But I've really made such horrible blunders". I say, "yes, but that does not give your blunders Godhood!" God has never abandoned His own Sovereignty because you did something foolish or stupid! He has never abandoned His post! -**He's God!** He knew what He was getting into when He made you, and again when He asked you for a relationship. In His own unknown and magnificent way, **He is perfecting His magnificence inside of the imperfect person you are**...but remember this: to Him you are already perfect!

He was always with you...Your meager mess-ups were never a threat to the perfection of Jesus on His Cross! Maybe you made a big mess, but He saw it coming. He wept with you and even now waits to bring you into a greater place of confident, fearless, and joyful trust. You see *"God was always in Christ reconciling the world unto Himself"* and He's tugging on your heart right now to **turn over** to Him that thing you're ashamed or fearful of. Do you trust Him? I believe you do! He is reconciling you and everything around you right now! Wow! A great new process is beginning. Yield the canvas of your life to the love of His Masterful hands and to the power of His Divine Brush.

NOW YOU CAN REPRODUCE WHAT YOU ARE!

Once you are surrendered to Him, He unapologetically goes for you heart. He is determined to set you free! When He does these things they ARE your New DNA! You will see yourself begin to reproduce these things in others. You can never reproduce what you aren't! But now you are His evolving Masterpiece! In Zephaniah God talks about how excited He was when you were born as He imagined all the possibilities. It's so much fun to reproduce ourselves. He has chosen you to Co-Create with His love and power! You are His own son or daughter now! You are His Ambassador on this planet living out your destiny in this life and you will be surprised at how your Father will create opportunities and bring together relationships where you are a "worker together with Him"! He has made you to be a *"minister of reconciliation"*!

He is Lord! May the Magnificence of His Love embrace you now as you read "Autographed" I can't wait for the world to read the Living Letter that you are, with all the Autographed experiences of your past and your goals for the future. <u>You</u> will be Autographed by none other than the One who is doing it millions of times over right now all over the world- Jesus!

BEWARE OF COUNTERFEITERS!

The Pharisees were religious leaders who did not buy into the sacrifice of God. They wanted to create their own salvation through their good deeds. They were masters of painting on their own canvas with their own religious ideas and then showing them off to everyone around them. They wanted to look religiously good in front of others. <u>The Pharisees were the epitome of counterfeit autographs</u>! They are a living example of those wanting to be autographed by their religion and their good deeds. This is why Jesus and even John the Baptist used such terse words toward them: "vipers, hypocrites, how will you escape the damnation of hell". Wow! Counterfeits are so dangerous because they present themselves as the real thing!...but they are indeed, <u>Counterfeits</u>.

Counterfeits are so dangerous; especially if they are leaders! When leaders are counterfeits themselves, they become the salesmen of forgeries! Literally, the blind leading the blind! What they offer is good-deed-doing in place of the real born again salvation that all people need! They indeed apply the most extravagant means to present themselves well...but they are indeed orphans with a well-rehearsed veneer.

> *"When leaders are themselves counterfeits, they become the salesmen of forgeries"*

We must heed the warning of Jesus, *"beware the leaven of the Pharisees which is hypocrisy"*. Leaven (or yeast) has the quality of growing in whatever bread dough it is put in. Jesus wisely warned us of this leaven-like quality of religious hypocrisy that masquerades for the real thing. *"You are whitewashed tombs full of dead men's bones"* Jesus thundered! Beware of religious masquerades! Beware of attempting to buy a place in heaven by doing good things. This leaven has multiplied all over the world through thousands of religions and truly has become the "opiate of the people". It has such an appeal to human pride! Even a good portion of the Christian faith has been tainted-even poisoned by this deathly leaven! Jesus told the Pharisees, *"Woe to you, teachers of the law and Pharisees, you hypocrites! You travel over land and sea to win a single convert, and when you have succeeded, you make them twice as much a child of hell as you are"*

Wow! Very terse words from a teacher of love!

THE REAL THING:

On the other hand, there are millions of true "Autographs" all over the world. These are other sons and daughters of the King. They are the imperfect family of God that is loved beyond measure by Christ and you are privileged to work with. You may even lead some of them!

They have a story to tell to the nations! They bear a message! That message is a man, and His name is Jesus! Scrutinize the painting <u>that they are!</u> Look as closely as you want. The Autograph is genuine! Look closely at the brushstrokes in the painting. Even the places in the painting where you see the "mess ups" of its' owner; you see the Autograph of the Master upon it! Nothing was overlooked. Everything is owned now by the King of Kings! *"There is therefore now no condemnation to them who are in Christ Jesus"!*

In the words of Martin Luther King Jr.
"Free at last, free at last, thank God All Mighty, I'm free at last!

No one can ever condemn them for those "mess-ups" because now they have the beautiful "write-overs" of the New Owner woven into them...and His signature over them! Jesus owns them! Now, look at the other Masterpieces of other's lives who have yielded themselves. Look as closely as you want! <u>His sovereign love has redeemed it all!</u> Every masterpiece has its own unique strokes, but look! Some of the strokes were intermingled with the strokes already on the canvas! No, it didn't make a mess like we might fear. It has become part of our fabric, our identity, our purpose, and our destiny! It even has become part of our dignity! Only God could do that! God has replaced our shame with His sovereignty! Strokes that once marred the masterpiece has now helped to create its uniqueness! As you observe the other Works of this Master, you see that this "Redeeming process" is one of His most unique traits. In fact, none of His works are without it!

What made the difference between a hopeless identity, a "leavened" forgery and that of breath-taking Creation? It is the touch of the Master! We are Genuine Autographs of the One Who rescued us!

But wait! Have you yielded? He reaches His hand to you right now! Take it! He must visit those areas <u>with you.</u> They may have happened years ago. They may have even happened when you were a teen...or a child! Trust Him! He must define them to you! Redeem them for you! He has already owned them for you on the cross. They can only be redefined by trusting Him. Release your grip on the brush! He must paint. I know you wonder how anything can be made meaningful about it. He will not doctor it up; neither will He scribble it out. It will be defined! It will be Redeemed! It will be owned by Him! It will even be...beautiful! *"He has made everything beautiful in its time. He has also set eternity in the human heart; yet no one can fathom what God has done from beginning to end"* Ecclesiastes :11

Can we join our hearts right now and Welcome Him right now and tell Him, "Jesus, I want only the best!" Let's determine right here right now. No short cuts! No areas of shame, pride, or fear will mar our lives anymore! Wholeheartedness will be the pilgrimage I pursue! My destiny is to be a Masterpiece!

<u>Let's pray</u>!

"Dear Jesus, I do not want to be an orphan with a dressed up veneer! Make me true! Possess me to the core of my heart! I release my grip on the brush. I trust you! I welcome you to work everywhere in my life. Here's my heart! I open it completely! Define me or redefine me, but I want you to completely redeem my life! I abandon myself to You! I want my love to be pure and my life to be without hypocrisy. I will not let others define me! I know my destiny awaits me, and I'm so excited! Lead me! Prepare me! Teach me! Make me genuine as genuine can be! I love You with all my heart! I want to grow in your grace and knowledge through this whole life I have on earth. Thank You Jesus! Amen

> *"God loves you just the way you are, but he refuses to leave you that way. He wants you to be just like Jesus"*
> *-Max Lucado*

A Dedication

I dedicate this to my kids, and to their kids! To my physical kids; to my spiritual kids; and to their offspring. Wow! We had a great time together! We were privileged to do great stuff, but most of all; we had the privilege of doing it together!

May you be blessed!

To all the families who welcomed me into their family and let me benefit from what Jesus has Painted into your lives, you helped make me what I am! Thank you! You gave me not only your time, but your lives.

Of all these, and more than any other, I dedicate it to my five wonderful Dobbelmann children, their wives and offspring-my wonderful grandchildren. You've added more meaning to my life than you will ever know!

Secondly, to the thousands whom I had the privilege of "leading into battle" i.e. the thousands who traveled on Mexico outreaches and to other nations with me carrying the Glorious Treasure of the Gospel within us as we went. To the many that looked to me as their spiritual father in Christ. Hey! We touched the world together! *"May God be glorified for the Wonder of His Son who is always conveying the fragrance of His Magnificence through our lives during our earthly existence."* 2 Corinthians 4:14

Chapter One

A Feat of Engineering Genius

The young mom's face and smile expressed her joy and relief that the labor was done and her baby was finally on the outside of her tummy. It had been a lot of work, but "it was worth it", she thought as this newborn's anatomy was on display to all those in the room in Swedish hospital that day. No, not in Sweden. But in Swedish hospital in downtown Minneapolis on June 7, 1949. This little vernix covered bundle of crying biology was not all that distinguishable from the others born that day, but the feat of engineering it took to get me there was unique. You see, I had an enemy; who, unlike my Loving Creator, did not "rejoice to see my day" and tried his best to prevent it

LIFE HAS AN INSIDOUS ENEMY

The enemy was (and is) called <u>"inconvenience".</u> This insidious enemy never seems to rest and never has the time of day for valuing anything human. It was a very inconvenient time for my mom to have a second child.

It was financially inconvenient. It was relationally and situationaly inconvenient. It was even relationally inconvenient. My dad was serving in the armed forces during and after WW2. To stay in the military was a safer

29

place to be than with the in-laws who still harbored resentment that said, "You got our daughter pregnant". My older brother was conceived out of marriage. Now, in those days, this kind of event strongly motivated the mom-in-law to get the knot tied. The problem was that after it was tied, it also permanently earned the mother-in-law's ire of what is now her son-in-law! So Elinor Coleman and Theodore Dobbelmann did just that and were wed before the birth of there first bouncing baby boy who was proudly named after dad. My dad soon found out that living under the same roof with the in-laws takes a lot of relational software that he just didn't have! So, he re-enlisted.

It was convenient for dad to serve in the military and mom to work at Kinney's shoes and live at home to save for the day they could buy their own place. Guess what? My dad comes home on leave during one of those "fertile" times and like magic, I'm conceived.

My mom realizes what an inconvenient time this is. She has a girlfriend who is pregnant at the same time who is also trying to earn money and begin a new life. Her friend discovers a doctor who does after hour abortions. For weeks she begs my mom to join her and go get the procedure. Finally my mom agrees, but is very nervous. So one evening they show up at the closed- to- the- public office hours of this doctor. The doctor greets them and assures them all will be well and mom's friend goes in first. My mom nervously picks up a Life Magazine to flip through the pages as she awaits her turn.

Then something happened to which I owe my very life. On the cover is a full page picture of Dwight Eisenhower's new baby. Whatever your politics, I owe my life to this kid! He's still alive at this writing. I should send him a Thank You! I owe my life to a picture of a president's baby! But more than that...<u>THANKS MOM FOR LIFE!</u>

I may not be a Billy Graham, Apostle Paul, or Superman, but I'm glad mom opted at the last minute to give me a crack at life! There are many who could have argued that maybe I should have been aborted, but I'm glad I was given the chance to try! The chance at life! Without a right to life, all other rights don't exist. I managed to dodge the abortionists' killing tools where many millions have not. I wonder how many we have aborted who would have invented the cure for a dread disease, or been another Billy Graham, or great inventor. When I hear that we have aborted more individuals than those who have died in all of our country's wars, I get scared that maybe our society has aborted important parts of its own future. Each of them was a specific plan of God, I tremble when I consider mankind's loss and the madness of deifying convenience. There is no higher and more regal work in the world than "kid raising"! What a chore, what an expense, but what a glory!

Someday I'll meet in heaven the little one who had to leave this life prematurely. That is, the baby of my mom's friend! I was so near that same doctor's knife that took that little one...just moments away from the same fate! I've asked God, "why it wasn't my mom who went first; maybe something would have stopped that friend from the procedure and that little one could have entered earth to realize his or her destiny! Why was I saved? I know he/she was embraced in the loving arms of Jesus. I'll meet that little one someday.

While on the subject of feats of engineering, how many of you have stories of your own near death experiences that God and His angels have "engineered" you out of! How about diseases, situations, or accidents that could have killed you? God watches over us each day and sends His angles as *"Servants to those who are heirs of salvation"*

> *"Even the smallest person can change the course of the future"*
> *- J.R. Tolkien*

How about how he engineered your dad & your mom coming together, or your grandparents meeting one another, or God saving them from death so you could be here!

My grandpa worked for over 40 years on the railroad. He called in only three times during his whole life. That was back in the time when you don't "call in", instead you "crawl in" to work! One of those 3 times that he couldn't even "crawl in", the train had a horrible wreck where the tracks were washed out on a mountainside in Montana. The train tumbled into a lake and the one who took my Grandpa's place was found dead, pinned under all the baggage in the train baggage car at the bottom of the lake. This was before my mom was conceived. You see, the Bible says; *"before Abraham was, I knew of you, and before you were ever brought forth, I knew your name"* Think of it! God has such a special purpose for you! His firm hand has guided you into your existence right now. And right now in this tiny portion of eternity called "our life span", God has a plan for you! Have you surrendered your life to Him? Have you received His forgiveness for your sin? What a waste if you were to be this close to fulfilling the destiny of your life and walking in the purpose for which you were made, and you mess it up! RECEIVE HIM! REACH OUT! LIFT UP YOUR VOICE AND CRY OUT TO HIM RIGHT NOW! The Apostle Paul said, *"I beg you not to receive the grace of God in vain".* You're in the middle of a tremendous and momentous thing-**your earthly life!**

Remember, you've been created by Jesus on purpose and for a purpose! No mistakes were made with you! Unlike the Evolutionist theory which, clearly stated could read, "From goo to you by way of the zoo"; Christ's statement about you is much more hopeful: *"Before I formed you in the womb, I knew you and ordained you to (fill in the blank)".*

What does God want to do through you during this time on the earth? You're a feat of engineering genius! It's time to release it! Like the Apostle John says, *"To as many as received Him, to them gave He **power** to become the sons of God".* This promise from God to reclaim you from your own demise and make you His own son came with the great price of His own Son paying the debt you could never pay! Now He adds to your own redeemed position of an heir and a son.

He continues reaching into your life to dress your life with the Royal robes of divine power! The marriage of His Presence with your personhood will become complete as you yield yourself to His Brushstrokes! Nothing can stop you from fulfilling your destiny! *"If God be for me, who can be against me"!* When you receive Him, it triggers the energy that launches your life into its destiny. Yielding your life to your Creator and Savior now births the Divine "Autographing" of your life.

We must guard the sanctity of all human life, because every person is created by God for a purpose. We are all created in His image. **<u>Abortion has never been about choice. It's about escaping the consequences of our choices by taking all the choices away from another human being.</u>**

Very few sacrifices in life are more noble and important than raising children. Thank God for the privilege! And, Thanks Mom for Life!

If Abortion has scarred your life, remember that it is not the "Unpardonable sin". Even more, it is not beyond the reach of God. He still loves you and, yes!..as you yield the brush to Him, He does far more than overwrite that part of you life. You say, how can that not be a shameful and marred portion of my life's canvas?" Oh, you have yet to discover the love and power of your Creator! If this is you, put the book down right now and take His hand. Now is the time for transformation!

Oh, here's a fun addendum to this story: you gotta hear this! The way my dad met my mom was in downtown Minneapolis. She had just been shopping and had her purchases in one of those paper bags with a handle on it. Just as he walked by, the handle broke! He, being the chivalrous man he was, ran up and volunteered to pick up the things for her. Think of this: I OWE MY LIFE TO A BAG HANDLE!!! God's got a sense of humor. You know, I can't wait to meet the angel that God dispatched to rip that handle!

I wonder how many angels were involved in preserving and guiding your life?

> *"This life is a dressing room for eternity!"*
> *-Leonard Ravenhill*

Chapter Two

Bona fide Union Labor

My grandpa would always point his crooked finger at us kids and remind us to vote Democrat...I think I was seven the first time he told me to do it! I wasn't gonna vote for another 12 years! He would say, *"You vote for Democrats because they're the ones that look out for the workin' man"!* I'm not making any political statements here. I'm not even making any value judgments on unions. I'm just telling you what happened. I was taught that hard work was the most important thing. The Union people would always brag about how important it was to use "bona fide Union Labor". I discovered that God made some "bona fide union labor" Himself. With all of their short comings, my Grandparents and parents were "bona fide union labor"...card-carrying members chosen from heaven! God was the Union boss...only without the corruption. He gave them to me to make me what I am.

My mom and dad got their wish, saved enough money, and bought their own home at 2305 Girard Ave. S. in Minneapolis in 1951. I was two.

I owe so much to mom's gentle encouraging spirit. She was also kind. She would even feel sorry for a worm getting put on a fish hook! She was true "Union labor" from heaven!

.She would tell us stories all the time. Each story would have a message about life. My favorite was "The 3 Little Fishies" that "fam (swam) and fam (swam) right over the dam" when they disobeyed their parents warnings about danger. These were the kind of stories that often did not have a good ending, but you always learned a lesson on life. Then there were the ongoing Sagas of "Jimadory and Jackadory" the good brother and bad brother that set examples of what to do and not to do. The right ways to live, and to help others

She didn't know Christ in a personal way, but was very religious. She dragged us off to Lake of the Isles Lutheran church every Sunday. When people ask me, "Did you ever do drugs?" I'll say, "yes, my mom drug us to church every Sunday". I often think if only some of the many pastors who she knew through her life could have shared with her the way to Christ how much my mom would have soaked it in.

Her beauty and fun carefree personality got her into trouble sometimes, but she loved life. Even during hard times she would have some song she would sing with a positive bent on life. I learned to be positive, and to endure, and even to sing from her example. She ran for Miss. Minneapolis and was very talented in acting, singing, and music. If she could have had more biblical wisdom she would have touched the world with these gifts. I now see her personality reflected in my sister and my daughter.

My dad on the other hand would not go to church at all. My mom would often threaten to send the pastor over, and he swore if he came in the front door, that my dad would go out the back door. When my grandpa emigrated from

Holland, he left the family's religion there. My dad was one of four sons and none of them saw value in religion.

Despite his distain for religion, my dad was wonderful. The days he was alive were the most secure of my life. I remember the days before he died when I was nine. There was a constant sense of security. Memories like being in the back yard in the '50's as my mom is hanging up clothes to dry; our Cocker Spaniel, Taffy, playing with me as I would hear propeller driven airplanes flying overhead.

My older bother, Ted, and some of my relatives would remember dad differently. To them he was insensitive, too strong, and even harsh. This was because they did not honor his strength. I respected it; they deplored it. To this day, I would say my mom almost worshiped it.

I would go for rides in the '51 Buick. He let me shift. He would bring me to his shop on 34th and Lyndale. I would try to memorize the route so I could ride my bike over someday by surprise. All his employees were "real men", right? They would greet my dad and me with something like, "morning Ted, hey, you brought the kid today, huh?" They towered over me. They would rub my hair and say, "what do you say?" I would always answer, "I don't know".

We would always go for rides. "Sunday driving" was popular back then. No one had cable and AC to go home to so we would take a drive. The whole family would go every Sunday. We lived in Mpls, the "City of Lakes". I would anxiously roll down my window and open the little "vent" window on my side. We would always drive around the lakes, visit the Rose Garden, and if we went to Dairy Queen, it never paid to argue with dad about what we would get. It was always the plain kid cone. Don't even bother asking for chocolate dip. <u>It didn't happen.</u> We loved it. Then we would stop at Sonny's Ice Cream shop. He would get ½ gallon of vanilla for the evening TV time. I do remember asking, "Dad, can we get this other flavor ice cream?" <u>It didn't happen.</u> We would go home and eat it in white bowls with Hershey's chocolate syrup and watch Lassie at 6PM. It was heaven. It was strength. We lived in confidence.

A trend today is that parents need to give kids what they need to be fashionable...and even give them what they want! A much more important thing is to do what my dad did: <u>know me!</u> Love me! <u>Be interested in me</u>! Include me in your life!

> *"It is a wise father that knows his own child"*
> *-William Shakespeare*

We would always visit his brother's place of business and I would listen to them talk ideas. I learned the importance of extended family, dreaming dreams, inventing new ideas, laughing, and how to just be relaxed with others. Ideas are always more important than image! Ideas are one of the unique and wonderful privileges of mankind. To have powerful ones, we must draw from a place of inner freedom, courage, creativity, and confidence. Image is what you worry about when you don't have the former! When you haven't prepared yourself for great thought, life is not very exciting. Great thinking comes from lives that are Autographed! One can finally transcend the limitations of personhood only when we are surrendered to something greater. The life of a mere man ends when we wholly abandon ourselves to Christ! The Apostle wisely put it like this: *"I am crucified with Christ, nevertheless I live, yet not I but Christ liveth in me..."* Galatians 2:20

> *"One can finally transcend the limitations of personhood only when we are surrendered to something greater than ourselves"*

Dads are a kid's super hero. How sad when we are too tied in knots to be a kid's hero. Being a kid's hero is one of the easiest things to do on the planet; as long as you begin early enough. Just pray that God would lead you, and then do it! My dad even had a medical condition that prevented him from doing things like boating, camping, and sports; but he knew me, and I was interesting to him!!! When you look at my Canvas, you can see all kinds of brush strokes from my dad!

I recently read the conclusions of a study about childhood relationships. It said that a child's IQ and his/her understanding of vital relationships (i.e. family roles, values, the place of grandparents, uncles, cousins, church life, and how God fits into our life, etc.) are largely determined by age 4!

I'm grateful for my dad's example in many of these areas. He is still my hero.

GOD PLANTS A SEED

God made up for dad's spiritual deficiencies one day. We were watching TV on a Saturday morning. Very few shows were on TV in those days so when something came on, you usually watched it. Oral Roberts came on with his healing crusades. As a small child, I was very moved by seeing crippled people getting up out of wheel chairs and throwing away their crutches. My dad and brother were sitting directly in front of the TV keeping the knobs adjusted for a good picture and laughing at this guy who was one of the first televangelist. They were putting him to shame. I was behind them on the couch. When Oral Roberts gave the invitation for the TV audience to give their lives to Jesus by raising their hands, guess what I did? How could I not? All I had was childlike faith! As I cautiously slipped up my hand so no one would see me, my brother looked around and saw me. He quickly said, "look dad, Darrell's raising his hand". They both laughed at me for doing that. My brother made up for it about 18 years later when he left his drug induced lifestyle and surrendered his life to Christ's' love and power. One of the first things he thought of was his long-haired lost brother. He came over and with the help of some friends, led me to my "born again" decision for Christ. I still look back at that Oral Roberts time and wonder if God some how "marked" me, because it seemed like after that time, I see the brush strokes of God on my canvas. I even felt like He would talk to me!

If you look hard enough, you too will begin to see how God did not abandon you during growing up. Sometimes it is so important to make a touchdown; God just takes the ball away from your parents and does it.

When I was 4, the big diagnosis happened. Dad had a heart valve problem from when he had rheumatic fever as a kid. Scar tissue had been growing over a valve and it was weakening him severely. That was in the days before they could replace heart valves. The only procedure was heart surgery that involved operating while his heart was running! And slipping a knife through a small incision above the damaged valve and by the surgeon's feel, to cut away the scar tissue. He was 36 and the procedure was a terrible failure and they cut deeply into his heart valve.

His health deteriorated rapidly. He had to sell his auto body business, and go on disability. We became poor. This young strong family man now couldn't work, couldn't be active with his four boys, and couldn't teach us sports. He couldn't even sleep unless he was on his knees in a praying position beside the bed hacking and coughing all night. I would wake in the morning and find the toilet full of blood that he had coughed up through another agonizing night.

I remember during that time, my older brother made life even a worse hell for dad by being rebellious and self-centered. In my dad's weakness, my teenage brother had no sensitivity to the importance of helping run the home. He would even make fun of his sickness, and laugh about him dying. If my dad could muster enough strength to discipline him, my brother would call my Grandparents who would then side with my Brother and make life even more miserable for this man. My Grandparent's drove a deep wedge into our family through this behavior. Even Union Labor can really mess up on some jobs! My dad got so little support at this difficult time. He never whined about it. He stayed strong all the way to his early death on his 41st birthday

I admired him. In fact, honoring him was sort of "automatic". If he was fixing a light or a switch or plumbing, I would park my self at a "ringside' seat and just gawk at him. I remember once he was fixing our old blonde "Muntz" TV. He had the back off and was soldering something in the high-voltage section with a match. He said to me, "Darrell, don't get too close, if I get a shock, I don't want it to pass to you". I thought, "Wow, he's giving his life for the TV!!!" He was my hero; a real bona-fide Union dad!

I remember once as I followed him out to lock the porch door before we went to bed. Some strange man was

41

crouched down by the stairs looking up at the second floor bedroom window. We rented out our second floor to college girls. Dad always would say, "Girls always are more responsible than boys"...hmmm, that's not so true anymore. Anyway, dad knew this was a peeping tom and said, "Who are you"? The guy said, "shhh". Dad said, "I'll give you a shhh" and bounded off the stairs in hot pursuit of this young man. He chased him all the way around the house and the guy leaped the back-yard fence into the alley not knowing that there was a 5 foot drop into the alley. He landed with a splat and dad pursued him down the alley. Needless to say, that night was an especially hard night for dad to breath, but God had put a brush stroke on my canvas about courage and defending your Home and Family.

He came from a Dutch background and always wanted his home simple and squeaky clean. I remember times he would come home and call my mom's attention to something he wanted dusted or cleaned. It was behavior like this that got him a reputation from relatives of being harsh. I just personally think the relatives were wimps.

Here's one more fun story! It came to pass that my mom wanted one of these new automatic washing machines. My dad didn't want to buy it. I remember that my mom sneaked over and bought a used one and had it delivered. It was one of those front loaders with a big window in front. You could see what was going on with the clothes through the whole cycle. When my dad discovered this machine, he said, "Elinor, what's this all about?" He got over it quickly and he pulled up a chair in front of it to watch this automated wonder go through its cycle. I pulled up a second chair to watch it with him! People were just more easily entertained back then!

After he died, my mom would often visit his grave...bringing poems and flowers and writing these words about his love, his strength, and his arms in her poems to him. I never knew my mom more content and happy than when my dad was alive. His strength set her free and she submitted to it.

I saw in my dad a hero. He conveyed the kind of strength I thought would be automatic when I raised my kids. When he taught me something, I listened intently. I envy his strength to this day!

> *"I cannot think of any need in childhood as strong as the need for a father's protection"*
> *— Sigmund Freud*

Chapter Three

The Day It All Changed

Sunday morning in 1958 my dad had the big Sunday Paper open to an article on a new machine that allowed surgeons to actually shut the heart down and take over the pumping functions. He said, "Darrell, come here". I quickly came over and crawled up in his lap. He showed me the pictures of this new invention and said, "This is my only hope".

Surgery was scheduled for a valve replacement. He was always optimistic. This continued right up to his surgery. My mom visited him the night before the surgery and was going to take home some extra candy bars that he had in the drawer. He said, "Leave them here, I want them after the surgery" On July 16, his birthday, He was operated on ...and died. My mom had stayed up all night reading the Bible and praying. What made it even more difficult was when the hospital called and said, "Your Husband is in the recovery room" Twenty minutes later they called and said, "I'm sorry Mrs. Dobbelmann; your Husband has passed away". I guess his heart stopped moments after the first call was made.

My mom was beside herself. She had four boys. One of them was a baby, and now she had no husband. At the funeral, my Grandparents literally had to carry her under each arm up to view the casket. She would go between crying and whimpering. I remember her taking my dead dad's hands, rubbing them and whimpering over and over, "Ted, Ted, Oh Ted". Some well meaning (but dumb) relative said to me and my 5-year old brother, "we'll, I suppose you're not really gonna miss your dad are you?" He was straining to be strong, but my 5-year old brother, Steve, burst into tears.

I remember standing beside the casket as a little skinny 9 year-old and thinking I had to take up his fallen torch of strength. I think this is where I resolved to lead my family some day when I got married. When I got saved years after this and started reading the Bible, it was great to read that God wanted all men to lead their families.

So many times when I was raising teens, I ached for a dad to call and say, "hey dad, what would you do if...." I remember the day that God wrote His Autograph over that part of my life. It's like God himself took my hand and brought me face to face with my tears, my lack, and my fear; but this time, God in His power was there with me!

It was in 1998 and my 3rd born son, Mike was making very troubling and painful decisions affecting the family. I was in prayer and again with a tear in my eye I was wishing I had a dad to talk to about the problem. God suddenly spoke to me and said, "Darrell the wound you have from not having a dad will always be with you". I responded, "God, that's not a nice thing to say, I thought you were a healer?" He said, "Your wound is healed, it's not open and raw, but it's a healed wound. You will always be able to see the scar, but now my autograph is written over that scar. Now, stop wanting a dad and start being dad to the thousands of teens I'm sending on bus outreaches to Mexico with you". I literally felt the hand of God Autograph that part of my life! I was suddenly unfettered from this orphaned feeling with all its hopelessness and pain. Now, instead, the experience became part of my strength for the future

It changed my life! It changed my ministry! I had a new confidence! The Mexico outreaches took on a new tone. We had to buy more buses, do more outreaches. Whole teen groups and hundreds of individuals began coming each year, and year after year with this type of testimony: "This is the most exciting part of my year", or "I feel like this is my family". As these people grew into marrying age, they wanted me to do the ceremony. Some joined our staff, became interns, and went into full-time ministry. Others became successful in business and support us today. Others joined our staff and started the Youth With A Mission (YWAM) base in Antigua, Guatemala. Jesus has autographed the wound of my dad's absence in my life and turned it into an asset of confidence and identity. Now it is part of my confidence and identity.

> *I literally felt the hand of God Autograph that part of my past! I was suddenly unfettered from this orphaned feeling with all its hopelessness and pain!*

Let me add that, with all of us, many of the things that hold us back happen very young! Often when we were only 4 or 5 years old! Every human being has survival as his/her strongest motivation. This survival (me) instinct couples up with our relational prowess to come up with solutions that are not very nice if we bring them into adulthood. Each of us figures out how to interface with others (usually to get our way), but at least to survive and be thought well of.

Often the skills we learn are things like:
> Throwing a fit!
> Acting out or Manipulation
> Shaming others
> Deception
> Ambiguity or Contrariness
> As we get older, we add defense reactions like "projection" and "denial"

Well, like Max Lucado says, God loves us too much to leave us like we are, so He applies His great powers of love, mercy, and grace to change these things and teach us biblical ways of "survival". In fact, as we grow in Christ, our confidence takes the place of the need for survival and our primary motivation becomes that of honoring Him!

If we loosen the grip on the paint brush of life, God gives us far better tools and habits wherewith to interface with our human family! He begins his masterful brush strokes of healing, forgiveness, and revelation of new things. He tremendously broadens our frame of reference and our confidence and our command of some pretty darn good new tools to use in this life! After we learn them, others stand up and take notice. People start coming to you for "counseling". You start hearing things like, "you have a lot of wisdom"...it's true! But it all starts with humbly acknowledging you were wrong, taking the Master's hand in trust, and facing those things that maybe even started many many years ago.

Most of us have been by the bed-sides and even the grave sites of those who have never allowed God to touch these deeper areas of their hearts! Though we get into heaven on Christ's "report card", what a shame to have wasted the one life that we have!

The Apostle Paul would often use the term "fear and trembling" in his writings. It was always used in the context of obedience. This was not a fear of God's judgment for disobeying; rather it was a sobering realization that Paul knew that he himself actually had the power to really mess up his own life by disobedience! He knew that he could miss out on all that God wants to do with him here on earth! He knew that he actually had within himself the capacity to do things his own way and thus miss out on all the freedom, wisdom, and confidence in this life that brings us into the next life. Our disobedience will never cheat us out of our salvation, but it cheats us out of the rewards and positions that God will grant us in the Heavenly Kingdom.

I've entitled this chapter "The Day It All Changed". Maybe this is the day it will all change for you! Is it time right now to put the book down, listen to the Holy Spirit speak to your heart, and allow some Divine brush strokes on your life's canvas. It starts with humility. It starts with "Jesus, forgive me, I was wrong..."

Well my mom took my dad's death hard; didn't eat, and worried for a few months, went down to 90 pounds, and then did the "pendulum swing thing" and went off the deep end. She started hanging around bars and bringing home some absolute riff-raff. All of the stability, and purity she had during my dad's marriage, she threw out the window.

A person is always somehow tempered by the mysterious ability to endure. God gave that to kids too! <u>But the pain and loss always becomes part of their personhood.</u> The question is, will it be a strength? Or, will it be a liability? One of my college Profs told me once, *"The same rays of the sun that melt butter can harden clay".* Like Joyce Meyer says, *"Adversity can make us bitter, or it can make us better!"*

We live in a day when people feel orphaned of love and they are like walking-wounded seeking refuges that instead turn into briar thickets where the wounds only deepen. This is what happened to my mom. We make decisions out of our pain, and our depraved nature joins forces with our survival instinct to come up with the most audaciously ridiculous solutions. We make decisions where our relatives say, "You're going to do what?"

Oh to God, that we may transcend that destructive black hole that seems to pull us toward it into destruction! May we somehow by God's Grace instead enter that room wherein we find light! Here's the paradox: Just as the doorways to destruction that the devil leads us into by labeling them "this way to happiness"; the real doorway to life has a threshold that reads "death"! Jesus said, *"If anyone desires to be my disciple, he must take up his cross daily and follow me".* It is one of the paradoxes of the Bible! Taking up your cross and passing through it is the only way where Jesus input can continue to define you! The devil will scream at you, "don't hang around those Christians, or don't give up that relationship, or don't let God at that part of your heart"

God is being straight with you right now. If you want a great life, something has got to die first! *"Whoever seeks to gain his life will lose it, but whoever loses his life for my sake and the Gospel's, that person will save it"* Mark 8:35

> *"The doorway to life reads, "Death". It is one of the paradoxes of the Bible! Passing through it is the only way to continue to have Jesus define you and refine you!"*

At the time, my mom was 35 and had been a beauty queen and even Miss Minneapolis in her younger years. She was still a great looking gal and had no problem attracting men with scummy motives. Even as a kid, I knew what their motives were. I remember not one of them having any interest in us kids. What a change from having a real dad, to now being around this male trash. <u>Nothing takes the place of a dad.</u> Oh how my heart ached for him to be with us again. I would go to his grave and cry, "daddy, come back".

The Bible says, "*Visit the widows and the fatherless in their affliction*". It is affliction! How I would have loved some dad-figure to come over and love me, but it never happened!

After a few years of this turmoil, my mom met a guy 15 years older than her. Bob C____. He was a wealthy General Mills executive who swept her off her feet because he actually worked, was successful, and had money. He would bring her to nice places to eat. She had never had this before. The others were low-class, & uncharactered scumbags. This one was a high-class uncharactered scumbag! She got pregnant and they quickly married. There was only one problem...he already had a wife and a family! So the marriage was annulled. Mom had my baby sister, Cheryl, in the government hospital. He didn't even provide a decent place for her to be born.

Finally my mom met a simple but decent man, Bob Lehse. He was a farm boy changed factory worker. She quickly saw he was the "pick of the litter" except he was 10 years younger than her. That was simple to remedy. Just lie about her age and hide or destroy every document that has your birth date on it...not a good beginning to a relationship! She pursued him and they were married in 1961.

This did not solve the hell we lived in. It seemed to broaden it. This new man could in no way mach our expectations. So, we did to him what my Grandparents did to my first dad...crucify him.

Crucifying family members never helps. Ask me, I've tried it.

We never called him "dad". I personally told him that he wasn't my dad. He grew up in a dysfunctional home himself and had virtually no relational wisdom or communicational skills. All he knew was how to get hurt, and give hurt. That's all I knew too.

When I turned 14, I started fighting him back. I hid in my basement room most of the time, but when I heard him beating my sister Cheryl, and hearing her appeals to not hit her, it was too much and I would blast out of my basement lair and try to stop the injustice by force. She represented my mom's past life, so he seemed to target her mercilessly. Sometimes, he would strangle my mom and once my brother actually sprayed pepper spray in his face. He just broke down and cried as he washed it out of his eyes. Such pain, such hurt, and no one having any relational wisdom from the Bible to help us deal with it---just "hurting people hurting people". I would go to my dad's grave again and cry. Oh, that someone could have introduced us to Christ and we could have experienced His Brushstrokes and learned the great relational wisdom from Scripture, but it never happened. We were all alone with our feelings, and offenses, and hurts; just hurting each other over and over again.

My mom would always hug me. Thank God. She never condemned me. She always believed in me. She never compared me to anyone else, or made fun of me like my Step-dad did. In fact, I don't think my mom had negative thought about me in her life. All the kids love her to this day. Even with all of her shortcomings, she won something in all of our hearts. Her unconditional love has never been in question.

She was not a practical mentor, however. When I got older I needed more than stories. Teach me motivation, teach me purity, teach me self-discipline, and teach me even how to brush my teeth!

There is a message here though. My mom just turned 93 and lives by herself. We all go over and cook for her, visit her every week, and take care of practical needs. I admit that she is getting a little persnickety in her old age, but every one of her kids still sends her at least a big card and sometimes brings flowers, candy or gifts on every Mother's Day and every Birthday. I'm not bragging, I'm just stating something that's amazing! She has done things where we could bear life-long grudges but instead we give her cards, kisses, and flowers! When I talk to the mothers whose kids forget these two days, I feel so bad for them! Often they have a tear in their eye. Most of them try to cover it with excuses like, "well, I know my kids are busy".

Let me speak to all of you who forget your parent's special days. I cannot fathom it! Please don't feel guilty, just change! The only commandment in the Bible with a promise is *"Honor your father and mother **that things may go well with you and that you may live long on the earth"**.* You will be hard pressed to find anyone who honors their mom and dad who doesn't have a blessed life! The best thing you can do in your own life to receive God's blessing on your life and success in your work is to "Honor your Father and your Mother"!!! Do it!

My mom had sooo many messes that she made. And her kids made sooo many messes themselves, but the one thing I never doubted was my mom's love. She never once shamed me in my entire life. Whatever I did, she loved me and spoke well of me. I'll introduce her to you someday. The first thing she'll do is give you a kiss.

My step dad passed away just few months ago. He had gotten saved, but there should have been so much more "Autographing" in his life! There was some autographing of Jesus right after his salvation, but then his old habits of unforgivness, and self-pity came back. They were like drab parties he would visit often. He never turned them over to Jesus. They were like thrones with dreary gods that he seemed to bow to whenever they would beckon him "come".

I'm grateful that my stepdad had a work ethic though! He also was faithful to my mom. These are the two foundational things to look for in a man before marriage. If a man lays down his life by working and stays morally faithful, those are the two legs a marriage can walk on! You can build on these. If he doesn't have these, there is nothing to build on!

Upon these two legs must be a love for Jesus, a life governed by His Word, (Psalm 1), and a determination to hang with the right people. My dad seemed to never realize that happiness is only 10% what happens but 90% how we look at it! If somehow my Father could have learned this as a child, Wow! How things would have been different! What freedom would have been His!

In his final months, he did love to hear God's Word and had a tremendous peace. WE would read him the Bible as he was dying and he would say "WOW, that's really something". Now he's with Jesus.

My mom's personality was the opposite of my dad's. I am grateful that my mom had the personality she did. She would sing during the hardest of times. The songs were always these upbeat secular songs with lyrics like "...lift up your head and shout, its gonna be a great day", or "you gotta accentuate the positive, eliminate the negative, give place to the affirmative, don't mess with Mr. In-between", or "never saw the sun shinin so bright, never saw things goin so right"...an <u>unbelievable quality of endurance! Thank God for a positive attitude in my mom. I learned how to sing during hard times, how to love unconditionally, and how to have a positive spirit from my mom!</u> Those qualities were foundational in my life!

I *"rise up and call her blessed"* to this day! Proverbs 31

I never had one friend during my teen years. My grades started to suffer. After all, who can concentrate on school in a situation like this? I had no friends, adult or peer. None! No one! For 4 years as a teenager I hid in my basement room from my dad and went to school and had not one friend. Kids would always pick on me in school until I just wouldn't care any more, and I'd blast one of them with my fist and he would leave me alone until another came along. Gym class was a place for all to mock me. I was always the last one to get picked when teams were picked. If this wasn't humiliating enough, as I was the last one picked, the one team would laugh as the other team "got stuck with me". Couldn't one person have had the character or the guts to disagree with those peers or take time out of their busy rituals to come up and say something kind to me? Couldn't one teacher have brought me to McDonalds and told me I was doing something good? Couldn't one Christian have knocked on my door and invited me to a youth group or a Bible Study or just sat down and told me Jesus loved me? Not one teacher, not one principal, not one pastor, not one family member, would put their arm around me or just look me in the eye and say some life-giving thing to me.

Remember that when you meet someone, they probably are not interested in the important theological positions you believe in, they probably don't care about the age of the earth or whether one political candidate is better than the next. They just want to be loved! They want to just figure out the purpose of their existence! The key here is respect! God gave you the privilege of meeting another member of the human race-created in the image of God, I might add! Meet their needs and then share with them your "witness". Acts 1:8 This is not rocket science. Just share with them what this man named Jesus did in you life! Then invite them into Christian fellowship. Love them! Love them! Love them!

Now with me, I still had an aching hunger for a dad's affirmation. As I pointed out, Scripture says the *"truest form of religion is to visit the widows and fatherless in their affliction"*. To not have a dad is the most grinding and identity-less form of affliction. Why don't churches make more of a ministry of this? We are living in a crisis time of fatherless homes...what should we do? Surely God can give us wisdom. OK, I understand how men have to work through the problem of single mom's to be a surrogate dad to their kids, but we can do it! And we can come up with some great women's ministry to these single mom's at the same time. Let's have a high summit! These people must be loved! Let the church of Jesus Christ answer the call! Lives are at stake!

Finally in 11th grade, my dad threw me out of the house and I quit school. I moved into the garage at the house where I grew up. My mom still had it as rental property and the garage was open. It somehow was the closest I could get to a sense of security. I lived there for months until the Minnesota winter started taking hold and I would shiver as I would try to fall asleep on the old sofa. One day, when I was away, someone broke in and stole all my stuff. So, out of desperation I went to my Grandparents. I remember my grandpa holding out his arthritic hands, welcoming me at the door, and saying, "my home is your home, and you can stay here as long as you want". Thank God for Grandparents! The months I spent at my Grandparents were life giving, and finally the lower apartment opened up at the original house I grew up in and so I moved in. I was trying to come full circle and come back to the only place that I ever had any identity.

Chapter Four

The Cloverleaf Twins

The Engine we just put into the 1954 Buick rumbled to life and we were both excited! We'd spent the last 3 days (and two nights) adapting in a 60's vintage 325 horsepower motor and a 30's vintage floor shift manual transmission into this 54 Buick. My cousin, Bill was so impatient to see how it performed that he blasted off down the alley without checking the coolant. I heard the powerful machine screaming around the neighborhood for about five minutes. Then it came back down the alley. Bill shut it off and got out of the car swearing. He had forgotten to put water in it! The grease on the engine was literally sizzling!

These kinds of escapades were common between me and my cousin Bill from about 1966-1969. His home had also become dysfunctional since his mom had an affair about 8 years earlier. She was unrepentant and it had really disrupted her relationship with his dad. His parents like my own had painted some pretty ugly things on their canvases of life, and when all was said and done, there was no recognition of wrong doing; only a blaming of the other.

Though Bill & I had known each other all of our lives, we sort of discovered each other for the first time on the basis of our dysfunctional parents and car mechanics. In fact, our love for old cars became our God. I was 17, both of our homes were dysfunctional, and we grew to literally worship 1954 Buicks. My cousin had four of them himself! I finally bought one myself, but my dads old 51 Buick was my main car. We became sort of a counter-counter culture that revolved around 1954 Buicks, Hostess Cupcakes, and RC Cola!

I think this life style developed because no life model was really presented to us by anyone else. We also found such a release in this lifestyle because of the hard lives we had had up to that point. Bill was two years younger than I and he couldn't see any reason for school either, but since he was only15, he was in constant trouble as he was trying to quit school before the state required age of 16.

Another part of our identity is we had two old Milkman delivery uniforms from the Cloverleaf Milk Company. We used these as our overalls when working on cars. We would ride small 20" bikes when our cars were unusable. It was hilarious to see us in our clover leaf milk costumes with our 6' plus frames on these small bikes and long hair blowing in the wind. We also never drank, smoked, or did drugs. Our only friends would be those attracted to our lifestyle and who chose to affiliate with us...and, attract them we did! Our counter-counter-counter culture actually began growing! Others thought we were cool.

My observation of this part of my life is that it rescued me from drugs, alcohol, and maybe insanity! Vices were rampant in our culture, yet I largely escaped them! I am actually grateful that I found my cousin and this life-style until I found Christ. The memories of this era are just fun!

If you want to skip over this part and go on to the next chapter, go for it, but I know some will get a kick out of it! I hope there is at least one part of your life that you can just laugh about. Here is mine:

A crucial part of any counter culture is their jargon. We sort of automatically developed a virtual dictionary of our own terms- we developed and used them in our every conversation. Once we got saved, our pastor even began using them!

First of all I never called my cousin Bill, "Bill"! I called him "Roc". He never called me Darrell; he called me either "Joe" or "Hairdo" I guess because of my long or strange hair. Then everyone in our counter-counter culture got a new name. I'll include those names along with other terms in the following short-list:

<u>Here's a short glossary of terms:</u>
Me ="Joe or Hairdo"
Bill ="Roc"
Our long hair ="The Curtain"
Bill's car ="the Century"
Our overalls ="Costumes"
Easy Chair in the garage ="The Back Breaker"
Roc's left hand which was damaged in a CO_2 Cartridge explosion ="The Clamp"
Roc's dad who would come out at 3AM and shut down our operations ="Pajam" (he would always break up our late night work in his pajamas)
Roc's mom ="Nighty" (she always wore one)
Our best friend ="Dopey" (he was a bit undereducated and always pronounced "L's" with "W's" and ended words with vowels

Big Buick Transmission ="Sixo Bewt" (the number of bolts on the top cover of this specific transmission, and pronounced like dopey would pronounce it)
Small Buick Transmission ="Fivo Bewt"
Our friend who brought us left-over donuts from his job at Emerichs bakery= "Donut man"
Our Lebanese friend with long hair = "Explosion head" (because his hair grew out, not down)
A later friend = "Mushroom"
My brother's friend = "X" (They couldn't remember his name)
My younger brother = "Poetz" (I have no knowledge of how this name was created)
Torque Tube style of rear axle commonly used in old Buicks = "Spikeball"-named after its appearance
Shop Foreman at our machine shop = "Mean Man" (he really was-I don't know why we kept going there.)
Our welder = "Doc" (like Bugs Bunny)
Proprietor at store where we would buy R/C Cola = "Heat Man" (His face was always red and the pop was never really cold)
Neighbor across the alley = "Cold Man" (His window A/C unit would run in the dead of winter)
Tarzan series on afternoon TV Matinee = "Ammies" (named after our favorite one, "Tarzan and the Amazons") which we would usually wake up in time to watch before we would start another work phase on cars

Afternoon host = "Jiggy Jiggleberry" (His real name was Woody Woodbury but he "Jiggled" when he talked)
Giving someone slack = "Leanage"
When you're having tough time with something = "I'm forcing it" or "it's a force"
When expressing a certain time, place, situation, or thing = "Those days"
The junk yard north of Cambridge, MN **or** A bad experience with a time place, situation, or thing = "Dumb Days"
The Junk Yard south of Cambridge **or** a good experience time, place, situation, or thing = "Neat Days"
That's all I can share in print. Someday I'll tell you more in private

Our passion for cars was so strong that sleep meant nothing. When doing some glorious engine transplant or transmission adaptation we would often stay up through the entire night ... sometimes more than one night. Our sleep schedule would be so weird that sometimes we would wake up and not know if we had slept a whole day or only a few minutes.

Bill's dad, "Pajam" would come out to the garage in the dead of night quite often and say, "Shut things down out here you guys, I've got to get up at 4:30". We would naturally keep going; just trying to be a little quieter. He would then come out and turn out the lights and say, "It's all done, nights over". We would be quiet for a while and just lie in the dark. Just work with a trouble light and keep the main lights off. Not use power tools, etc. But you know how it goes, eventually we would use more power tools, lights would go on and we would work through that night and into the next day. Sometimes even through the next

63

day and into the next night. Then we would fall asleep on the concrete for a while and wake up and keep working.

Permit me to use the aforementioned glossary of counter-culture terms to finish this chapter with some stories of those times!

One time we were working into a 2nd morning after being awake for two days with no sleep and I started hallucinating. I was looking at a Motor Manual getting some specs on something and suddenly I was on Mars and the words were written in Martian and made no sense to me. I came out of it and Roc's body was under the Spikeball. I thought he was dead. I said, "Hey Roc"...then louder, "Hey Roc!" He responded, "Yeah". I said, "What happened", he said, "I had these weird dreams <u>and then</u> fell asleep". Sometimes one of us couldn't resist having a downtime and would fall asleep in the "Backbreaker". It was great fun for the other to sneak out of the Garage and leave the other to wake up hours later with a sore back.

Whatever time we would go to sleep, we would always try to wake to see the Ammies and Jiggy Jiggleberry. We would rob Nighty's fridge, make bacon and eggs, watch the shows, and then Donut Man would come over with these huge boxes of donuts and rolls. By then, it was time to eat supper and start working on cars again until the next morning.

These cars had so much power that we could "Light up" the tires in second gear for over a block. Tire smoke would somehow come into the passenger compartment between the headliner and windshield. We were able to acquire tires for only $1. at "Neat Days", so even though Bill didn't have a job, he could afford to burn down these tires. We would use the wrong speedometer gears (the part in a car that enables your speedometer to convey the accurate speed) so the speedometer would appear like we could go 80 in first gear and 120 in second and so on. We would tell passengers to look at the speedometer as we "Floored it". The car really was fast, but with this added illusion of speed, it was really impressive...especially when the car is filled with smoke, and we're supposedly shifting into third at 120 mph on a city street, and the roar of the motor through those Walker glass pack mufflers that were under our feet contributing to the experience

One of our favorite "show-off" places was at Fuller Elementary school during recess. The playground faced a steep hill. When Bill would "light them up" on this hill, the tires would smoke forever because traction was not easily obtained, and since "Century" didn't have the ability to gain speed, the tire smoke would pour through the gap by the headliner so thick that we could hardly breathe. The kids would even be coughing after the whole escapade.

One time before going to this favorite place, Bill showed me two problems on the "Century" (Bill's 54 Buick). He walked me to the right rear of the car and showed me that the entire rear fender had rusted around the seams so bad it would literally wiggle. He pointed out that he needed to do some body work very soon. Then he showed me his right rear tire. It was almost bald. It had lots of tread when it was purchased, but it did not hold air so we put a brand new $3. Inner tube in it to make it inflate. Well, we always got our tires at junk yards for a dollar and had them mounted for another dollar, so for two dollars we would have a good tire to burn down. This tire was a special price because of the amount of tread remaining, but it needed a new tube in order to hold air. This $3. for an inner tube was a huge unexpended expense and we definitely wanted to protect that sizable investment! To do so, we had to not let the tire burn through to the tube otherwise the $3 tube would be ruined. He

65

pointed out that day that he had already burned through to the cord and said, "whew, one more burn and this one comes off...gotta save the tube".

So off we went to Fuller Elementary on the hill. All the kids came out and wrapped their little grade-school fingers through the chain link fence and began chanting, "Go Bill, go Bill". He revved up the mighty engine and dropped the clutch. The tires started pouring smoke off of them and tire smoke started to pour through the opening between the headliner and the windshield. The motor was roaring; the smell, sound, and sight of the power was glorious. The kids were all shouting, "yeahhhh". Then, like a drop of a huge hammer, there was a loud explosion followed by a crash. Bill's worst fears were realized. His prized tire had blown and ...oh no...the spendy inner tube came through the hole, grabbed a hold of the rusty fender, and literally tore it loose from its rusty moorings and flung it against the school wall. Bill stopped the car; all of the kids were roaring in laughter, he walked over to his fender, grabbed it, and threw it sideways into the gaping hole into the trunk. Then he drove away. Ka thumpa thumpa thumpa" on the blown tire.

Quite a day of humiliation.

Oh what I'd give for a video tape of that very event

It was a shame to have our relationship drift, but eventually Bill's desires for life parted from mine and we went our own ways. I am still grateful for those years and for Bill's friendship that was such a reprieve from my lonely life and an oasis from my misery.

Chapter Five

Monkees or Morons?

Put on your "I-don't-believe-it" seatbelts and let's go for another ride!

Bill and I found a fascination for putting on "way out" hippy type clothes those rare times we would take off our clover leaf costumes and wash the grease off of our bodies. We had this special place on Hennepin Ave. in downtown Minneapolis that we would buy clothes: striped bell-bottom pants, ruffled flare-sleeved silky shirts, homemade peace signs around our neck, and "Beatle" Boots. We would comb through our long silky hair, put on these clothes and go out for a ride. Sometimes some of our counter culture friends would dress the same and go with us.

One of these times we were hanging out in the alley chumming with some neighbor kids when one of them named Rusty with this really red hair said, "Did you guys know the Monkees are coming to town"? (For those of you lacking in years, the Monkees were the most popular Rock group of the era.) I looked at Roc with this devilish smile and we pulled Rusty aside and said, "Shh, don't tell anybody, but <u>we</u> are the Monkees! Now don't tell anybody; you promise?" Rusty said, "Oh nooo, I won't tell anyone".

The next morning Bill's mom woke us up and said," there are hundreds of teenagers all around the house and they think the Monkees are here". Roc and I got up quickly and woke up my brother Steve ("Poetz"). We quickly donned our best hippy dress-up clothes and strategized some "mini appearances" to tease these teens. When we first peeked out of the curtains we could only go "whoooa". There were teenagers everywhere-mostly girls. If they saw us peak out of a curtain, they would yell, "they're over here!" and all would come running and screaming to that part of the house.

We each quickly adopted the character of a band member. I was Mike Nesmith the guitarist, Roc was Peter Torq the drummer, and Poetz became the bands' heart throb, Davie Jones, because he could talk in an English Accent. We would peel back a drape just a bit and show the side of our face, a sleeve, or a Beatle boot and set off the screams. Steve would talk in his British accent and we'd here them scream, "I hear Davie talking".

Well, my aunt got tired of them trampling her flowers and threatened to blow our cover, so we created a strategy to lead them away from the house. We decided to lure them all to the front door with another of our drapery peep shows and then to charge out the back door and run to "the Century" (one of Roc's 54 Buicks) which was parked at the end of the block. We exploded out the back door and a few of the females that were out there yelled, "They're over here and they're getting away". We ran flat out and thought we had totally ditched them until I dropped my comb as I was combing my long hair while I ran. I reached down to get my comb off of the street and suddenly girls were pulling at my clothes. I broke away and charged toward the Century, I got in and locked the door as dozens of girls gathered around the car. I heard comments like, those aren't the Monkees", but Rock had to honk the horn ferociously and race the motor to get away. It was actually a bit of a dangerous situation. We left for a few hours and when we got back there were only a few souls around; only the die-hard true Monkee believers. We just let them know the whole thing was a ruse.

Ok, I'm going to be profound in a moment, but first let me share how much I learned to laugh in those days. It was such a joy! And such a change from my former life. It was so cleansing to laugh! Though my relationship with my cousin eventually parted ways, I will be forever grateful to him for helping me to laugh!

A historian wrote, "A nation forgetting its' own laughter is in a sad state of affairs". May God help us to renew innocent fun, & crazy laughter!

I'm grateful to remember mine, and pray to live it everyday.

In a different way, I think of that "Monkee" time and hope we never live out an image which we are not. We may not be Monkees, but often we convey to others a person that we are not. Most of us have an array of masks we don for various situations, but usually favor a few special ones: i.e. the "life-of-the- party" mask, "the strong-man" mask, the "I'm-self-confident" mask, or maybe the intellectual mask. Inside we're competing with others (and maybe competing with others' masks!) to escape the loneliness or brokenness or insecurity in our own core. Many have abandoned the idea of "living their core" years ago, as a bad idea; and so they live, day after day, living out a life that doesn't exist, ever wanting and never satisfying the great need of us all-<u>to just be loved!</u>

Here's a novel idea: develop your core!

DEVELOPING YOUR CORE

Here's the secret: It's a paradoxical thing I discovered it shortly after coming to Christ. Read this carefully: <u>You don't need a well-developed core to be self-confident. You only need a "developing core"!</u> That is now made possible because your identity is not a roadblock to self-confidence anymore.. The "developing core" shows that you have finally abandoned the lonely road of projecting images and you've breached the barbed wire of fear that used to tell you that you must find your identity in yourself! It is so liberating to be finally free of the worst tyrant that ever stood against me...me! Now we can say with a jubilant victory cry, *"I am crucified with Christ, nevertheless I live, yet not I but Christ lives in me; and the life I now live in this body I live by faith in the Son of God who loved me and gave Himself for me"*-Apostle Paul.

> **"It is so liberating to be finally free of the worst tyrant that ever stood against me ...me!"**

Truly, "<u>I am</u> the righteousness of God in Christ Jesus". That is my identity! Yeah!

Wow! Christ reigns in His identity inside of me! What freedom it is to not have to live out a life that isn't really mine to live anyway! *"Christ <u>in me</u>, the hope of Glory!"*-

In the sixties generation that I was part of, my peers began to discover how weary it was to project images and there was a great rebellion against our parents moors. There was a great desire to "just be me". There was not a ruder, more selfish, self-involved generation in the history of our land! You see, they missed the main thing. The only thing worse than "projecting image" is to "project depravity"! They had not heard the truth of Paul's words: *'In me, that is in my flesh, dwelleth no good thing"*, so they threw off the social mores of their forefathers and donned their t-shirts which read, "The freedom to be me"...and what yuk filled the land!

The doorway to "un-yukking" always has a threshold that reads death! It takes faith to cross it! Here is where being born again makes me a new creation where I can finally be free from a life of groveling in the dust for pebbles of identity, and to stop fighting with others over the pebbles that they have found. No longer is there a shortage of the "warm fuzzies" of recognition, well-being, and personal identity! The vastness of the sea of God can now be tapped to satiate those thirsts; and the wonder of it is that He fully satiates them without us ever pursuing them! <u>We buy into a thing called faith!</u> We hook our anchor on a completely different star! One that says, *"God is a rewarder of those who diligently seek Him" Hebrews 12:6* . No more seeking for crumbs that may fall from society's table; now I <u>am</u> *"an Heir with Father God and joint Heir with Jesus Christ His Son"*

Now, in front of me loom boundless treasures of God himself. This becomes the dreamed-for "third option"! Something beyond projecting an image that I knew wasn't me, and so much better than projecting the depraved "yuk" inside of me which should never be an option anyway! We don't have identity because we are born into a good family, but neither is identity found by redefining what it is and letting this personal redefinition take its place! The sixties generation was right to reject the counsel of their parents: i.e. to, in essence, live out a life of someone they were not. The mistake was to remove the façade of their parents only to reveal the disheveled core of their own souls! They should have abandoned the façade and then been born again into a new core! And then to build on that core with fresh new wonderful indelible ever-lasting truth from the Bible.

By beginning an adventure of seeking after God and seeking truth in His Word, we build our core! We actually begin to own something that formerly was light-years beyond our reach! Now, as the sons and daughters of God, our Father makes us heirs of things we can't even dream of, and gives us *"all things richly to enjoy"*.

The real ironic but great thing is that with this fear gone, we're finally able to do the things that develop our core! We seek Truth apart from self. This is where real discovery and freedom take place. In fact, we learn and become free at light speed! Then we integrate the things we learn into new thinking patterns that attract the intrigue of others. That leads to influence, leadership, and confidence. As we embrace real honest-to-goodness-eternal truth that we have found in the Heart of Truth's Creator, we can put those nuggets of truth in our own pockets and own them! We become seekers, thinkers, confident articulators.

When we're wrong, it only refines. As our hunger grows and our excitement soars at our new discoveries, we realize that our identity is not found in being right or wrong anymore. It's not even found only in what we know, but in our hunger to know more! This paradox is one of the great gifts God gives us. Its revealed in Mark 8:35: *"If you seek to keep your life you will lose it, if you lose your life for my sake and the Gospel's, you will find it"*

It's after our total surrender to Christ that we finally have the "muscle" that the world calls "self-confidence".

Now we are not limited by our fears anymore and we can really change, learn, submit, be accountable, and even question the basic principles of the world view that have governed us. We can compare it with the Bible, and through the leading of God Himself, we become true seekers of permanent, immutable truth that was here-to-for unavailable to my puny thinking patterns. It now becomes part of my confidence, my determined outlook, and my interface with others.

An identity that never existed now rises from the ashes of my former life. The governance of God's reality begins to sustain me and motivate me and guide me!

I would now be wise to abandon what scripture calls "futile thinking"! Personalized truth is something that mere men cloth themselves with to prop up their frail egos and temporal mindsets.

I will now begin to mine the real Gold gifted me by the Creator! I now have access to the very source of Truth! The question is will I search it out of God's Word? Will I incorporate it into my actions? Will I teach it to my children and grandchildren?

Welcome to the place where Ultimate Truth is applied by the Creator's loving hand to your life! The Brushstrokes are breath taking. The movements of His hand transfix you. The Masterpiece that is being formed right in front of you is your own life, and you are Autographed!

Chapter Six

The Miracle Wig!

"We're giving you a raise and making you a foreman, Darrell. We think you're doing a great job". Wow! A short while after I started hanging with Bill, I got my first real job. My sweet mom found it for me, because she couldn't afford letting me live in the duplex for free, and it was one of the best things that ever happened to me. Finally there was authority in my life that I respected. Bob Strom was the vice president and he "discovered me". He saw I had a knack for everything mechanical, hydraulic, and electric. My ability to learn seemed absolutely endless. It was just the way God made me! He even discovered I had a knack for people skills and the company trained me and gave me opportunities to learn, grow, and lead.

My grandpa taught me two things that have been life-saving. One is monetary wisdom; the other was respect for your boss. He told me, "When you get a job, Darrell, make sure you do things however that boss wants them done". I realized my boss wanted things done quickly and professionally, and with high quality; so I practiced everything I could, to be the quickest and most professional person in the plastics industry. I would stay after and read Tech Manuals on the machinery and on the qualities of plastics and their processing. One time the president saw me reading a Tech Manual long after quitting time. He said, "We really appreciate you getting so proficient in this stuff, but if we pay you overtime, then others will want it for unassigned stuff too". I told him I had punched out long ago. I was studying on my time.

It was literally like a new life! I had money, I had respect, I had the whole company behind my decisions, people wanted to be on my shift so I could be their foreman, they kept giving me raises until I literally began turning them down. I had so much money; I didn't know what to do with it all. The boss begged me to buy a new car. I could have paid cash for it and he knew it. Instead I drove my dead Dad's old 1951 Buick until it literally rotted out. It was one of those connections I needed with the past and with the man I thought I had to emulate. I did however buy a number of old classic cars. One of them was...you guessed it...a 54 Buick! It was a 54 Buick Skylark. The rarest 54 Buick in the world! It was their 50th anniversary car and only 860 of them were made! I owned one of only 4 that were licensed in the state of Minnesota! Years later I would use it to court my wife, Ellen, and it became our honeymoon get away car when we got married.

Ok, let's get busy with the substance of this chapter! You'll never believe this. A <u>wig</u> helped me achieve all this success. Say what? I'm not kidding. When I applied for the job I had my hippy long hair (the curtain) and the boss said, "We'd like to hire you Darrell, but your hair is too long for this work, if you get it cut, you got the job." I went home and pondered the situation. My hair was a huge part of my identity. Getting it cut was not an option. I had not cut it in 2 years and ended up going 5 more years before I did! Then a light bulb went on under my hairy head! I looked in the yellow pages, for wigs. I found a place that could trim down a woman's elastic wig, and I could tuck my long hair underneath. I did it. I was impressed! It sort of looked like a Beatle cut. I went back to Olson Tool Co. for the job. The boss looked at it and said, "well, how about a little shorter?". I said, "Look Bob, how about if I promise that my hair will never be longer than this". He said, "Ok" and I got the job. It never did get any longer. It was an easy promise to keep. Wigs don't grow!

"NO WAY" WIG STORIES

It's laughter time! I have numerous hilarious stories about that wig that I worked in for 5 years. I'll just share one for brevity. I was called in to do maintenance one Saturday morning in February. I got into my prized 1957 Chrysler (I had now graduated from Buicks) It was very icy road conditions and I reminded myself to be cautious. While entering the freeway, I looked in my rear view mirror and saw this young lunatic following me and fish tailing his car trying to get by me...on the entrance ramp! As he passed me, he lost control and hit my rear which sent us both spinning. Round and round we went. As the spin was slowing, I thought I was going to roll out of his way just in time, but no; he nailed me in the right rear. He hit me with such force that my Chrysler flew unto the side off the road. The force was so great that my wig flew off. Now underneath my wig I wore the top part of a women's old Nylon stocking...it kept my long hair up good for me to slip my wig over. I kid you not, and it keeps getting funnier. As I got out of my prized vehicle, all I could think about was yelling at this guy. I wasn't even aware that I got out of the car with no wig...just a Nylon! He approached me with silver dollar eyes and said, "Oh my G__". He thought the force of the impact had scalped me!

Oh, what the heck. I've got to share another wig story. I worked with a guy named Joe Brick. His brother married a gal named Betty Block...but that's another story. Joe was my set up man and the hardest working guy I ever knew. He made me look good as Foreman because of the productivity of our shift. When I was given a raise, I would go into the boss and thank him, but tell I didn't really need it. I have enough money, so please give it to Joe. Joe and I had a great working relationship.

We didn't compromise the productivity and quality one iota, but when we had time, we would play pranks with one another. One day while I was precariously balancing this $10,000 injection mold on one of its ends as I was cleaning it, Joe put an electrical wire around my neck and started strangling me with it. I was in a very vulnerable position because I couldn't protect my wig. I couldn't free my hands from the mold to guide the wire of my head. I knew when Joe pulled it off over my head that it could pull my wig off, and the fact that I wore a wig was one of the few secrets I kept from Joe. Well, my worst fears were soon realized. Joe pulled off the wire and my wig whisked through the air and fell on the shop floor. Again, all I had on my head was my bobby-pinned nylon and he thought he scalped me too! I quickly picked up my toupee and headed for the bathroom and insisted to Joe that he follow. Once there, I "reinstalled" my wig with Joe looking on in confused disbelief. All he could say was "gaaalll Dobbs, what the h__ is going on"! As he started to get the drift (i.e. that his long time boss and buddy wore a wig) he started laughing. I told him, "Joe, you can't tell anybody, ok"? He replied, "Oh, sure Dobbs" (with a smirk on his face that said otherwise).

Another time the boss & I were working on a piece of cooling equipment. He was especially frantic because this piece of equipment was failing and if it "went down" then five production machines would go down with it., We were both moving very quickly, I stooped over to check a line, and when I got up I hit my head with great upward momentum on the steel corner of a large flip-out open window. He saw the event and thought that I was mortally wounded! He said, "Are you bleeding?" I said, "No". He said, "Are you all right?" I said, "I'm fine". In disbelief, he said, "Let me look". You can imagine how I didn't want him to look! I quickly pulled my head away from his ever nearing scrutiny. Putting my palm on my head and pulling it away, I said, "See"! I always was cautious about people seeing the top of my head because the wig was cut down so far that the netting was very visible on the top. In fact, one day someone was working above me and glanced down and said, "Hey Dobbs, did you have surgery on your head"?

Ok, I'm on a roll. This is the last one...I promise! Another time I had climbed to the top of a 7 foot high stack of plastic pellets bags to connect an airline. The air hose was the quick connect kind and as I took my hands off of it thinking it was connected, I found different. It suddenly came disconnected with a "whoosh" and it blew the wig right off of my head. A toolmaker standing by said, "Dobbs are you Ok?" I quickly jumped down the seven foot vertical tunnel in the plastic pellet bags to grab my wig. All the time the toolmaker is saying "hey, Dobbs, Dobbs, are you sure you're ok, what are you doing?" I quickly put on my wig at the bottom of this 7 foot tunnel. I struggled to crawl up the 7 foot tunnel in the dark; and afterward I was greeted by the toolmaker saying, 'oh, you are ok".

Well, the next day, Joe told that toolmaker about my wig, and the jokes never ceased from that point. They called me the "Hippie".

FINDING MY IDENTITY

There were a few months after I got saved where I still wore the wig at work, but I would put it on when I arrived and take it off when I left. Then after 6 months I got my hair cut. I remember the place the Lord spoke to me about getting it cut...after 7 years! It was as I was turning right on 22nd and Hennepin. The Lord said, "Tomorrow you're going to cut your hair". I had total peace about it the next day as I saw those foot long locks falling on the Barber shop floor.

After I got it cut I thought to myself, "all these years I kept my hair for my Identity, but I concealed my identity with a wig"!

My Father in heaven has shown me so much about Identity since that time. Especially with my years with Youth With A Mission I learned that our love for other people-groups dictates often that we give up our personal preferences. We call it "surrendering rights". Long hair is not a sin. I would often defend it by saying, "It's my right!" It was! It's just like we have a right to things like preferences in clothes, jewelry, beverages, food, behavior, etc.

In 1 Corinthians 9 Paul talked about his right to the title of Apostle, his right to take a wife, his right to make money off of his ministry, but he said he would be willing to surrender any of these rights to "become all things to all men so that by all possible means we can win some"

Our identity should not have its final rooting in "rights" anyway! What am I saying? I know to some of you, it's a huge paradigm shift! Please don't dismiss what I'm saying like I'm nuts. I've found that some of the most beautiful strokes of my Creator were when I surrendered my rights to the food I like to eat to the food of another land, or to lay down my rights to my comfortable bed to sleep on a lumpy mat, or lay down my right to health as we reconstruct a culture after a natural disaster, or even lay down my right to life by sharing the Gospel to soldiers in a war-torn land. May I suggest to you that we cannot even find our identity in something as precious as our God-given rights? That's what Paul was saying in 1 Corinthians 9! That's what Jesus said, *"Even the Son of God (Himself) did not come to be served, but to serve and to give His life as a ransom for many."*

Here's a question for you to ponder: could you find a deeper identity in the joy of personally laying down God-given rights in order to bond with people of a different culture, or a different economic class, or a different living condition than what you're use to? Laughing and talking with them as we share food, fun, and fellowship together? I just returned from a remote area of the state of Orissa in India. While there, I was eating with my fingers (of my right hand) and laughing and discussing things. A few of the leaders looked at me and said, "We have never seen an American that seems as relaxed and enjoying himself as much as you". I told them, "That's because I <u>am</u> relaxed and enjoying myself".

A great book to read on this is "Making Jesus Lord" by Loren Cunningham

> *"It's great to not let our preferences create barriers to the wonders of the world's cultures, peoples, and it's customs. Relinquishing our rights is more often than not, <u>the only way</u> we can build bridges to other people"!*

We all love our countries, and have a right to our type of food, clothing, comfort, jewelry, entertainment, and customs. We can always come back to them, but we can't always find the opportunity to sacrifice them! It is so liberating to find our identity in something other than ourselves <u>and our preferences</u>! Paul says", *I am a debtor to the wise and the unwise, to the Greek and the Barbarian*". It's great to not let our preferences make limitations to the wonders of the world's cultures, its peoples, and its customs. Relinquishing our rights is more often than not the only way we can build bridges to other people!

Is there value here; especially considering that life is so short? Could there be a greater joy than just wanting things the way <u>we</u> want them?

We sort of get stinky and hard to live with when our bed, our food, our time, our clothes, and our customs all have to be just the way we like them.

Paul said, *"I beat my body and I make it my slave..."* Speak to your body! Don't let it dictate your decisions! Even things as wonderful as our rights need to be spoken to! Let your "rights" know that <u>even they are not in charge</u> of our lives. This will cut you free to behold some of the most beautiful strokes of the Masters hand on the canvas of your life!

May Heavens blessings be upon you as you find the joy of *"becoming all things to all men so by all possible means you can save some"* May His peace and power fill you as you *"esteem others more highly than yourselves."* May God give you **Grace** and empower you to build bridges to reaching others while having more fun than you ever thought possible.

And after that, to hear, *"well done thou good and faithful servant; enter thou into the joy of the Lord!*

Chapter Seven

Green Bugs and Politics

A box of church envelopes came in the mail. Somehow, the church I _hadn't_ attended in years found my new address. This was the church I grew up in. I was offended! They had the audacity to send me envelopes! I'm suppose to give money to this organization that never once helped us, even a little bit during all of our family dysfunction...what hypocrites! By what value system could such a thing be justified! How I would have loved to have had one person show me love...visit me...talk to me during those lonely painful years when I didn't know my right hand from my left. I threw the envelopes in the garbage and resolved that churches were not the place to find truth.

The house that I grew up in with my dad opened up, and I had moved in. I had my dad's old decaying 51 Buick, my good job, my wig, my thousands of dollars under my carpet, my classic cars, and was still enjoying my antics with "Roc", but I had a void in me as big as the Grand Canyon. There is a time in every man's life when he looks at his life and must say, "There has got to be more!" Like, something more than dope, more than drink, sex, and parties. Or in my case, more than money, success, cars and a good job! After dismissing the organized church as hypocritical, that inner drive led me into Eastern religions, philosophies and even into politics.

I got into Transcendental Mediation, Astral Projection, and the Guru Maraji. I got black lights, a sound system, posters, books, and these sound-sensing "thingamajigs" that flash different color lights. The music back then took some figuring out. The lyrics were abstract to say the least, and it was very fashionable to try to figure out the real hidden meaning. Then you get together with your buddies; smoke dope, and reveal the deep secrets that you've discovered.

I had many chances to do dope and never did. There was plenty of chances to fornicate, but I never did! Sometimes I attribute this to that decision I made at the Oral Roberts telecast years ago. At any rate, I am so grateful for the pain and destruction that that avoided! The ironic side of the pride I took in my eastern religions is that I prized my mental discipline so highly that I would say that I can have any experience "dopers" can have with just my meditation. To this day I can't believe I escaped drugs and sex. I certainly did not escape Demons. They would tantalize me with spiritual experiences and torment me with fears and manifestations.

My housekeeping skills were nonexistent. Stuff was all over my floor. Dishes stayed in my sink so long that green things that looked like bugs were on them. I would joke that they had eyes and would peek over the side of a dish! I remember becoming so frustrated with not having a place to sit at the kitchen table; that I took a broom handle and pushed all the dishes and trash unto the floor, breaking many things. I told myself, "from this time forward I will always have a place to sit down and eat". I actually kept that promise! A journey of a thousand miles started that day. My housekeeping skills improved from there.

I remember the things that the Devil sent along to derail me, but I know that I had a Supernatural Helper that kept me on track! The first was this sweet gal across the street that always tried to suck me into an affair. One time she called me crying at 2AM and said she really needed to see me. When I showed up at the door she had a suggestive see-thru thing on! Another time a gal came up to me and raised her dress and asked if I wanted a date. She had on these orange panties! Somehow I walked away from those invitations. Even when I was 12, I remember hearing the voice of the Lord say, "I don't want you looking at girls in their swimsuits". This was tough since I was coming up on summer and I was entering my "puby" time. God's word to "not look" saved me from those normal male addictions and possibly helped save me from affairs which I had plenty of opportunity to get into. I learned the biblical counsel to "flee fornication". Run from it! Immediately! Don't think about it. Don't even pray about it! **Just Run!**

Another profound time of hearing the voice of the Lord was when He told me as I sat at the dining room table when I was 21, "I'm going to give you a gift so you can help people". This was two years before I got saved! How did I hear God then? Well, maybe God knows those who will be "heirs of salvation"? I don't want to write any theology here, but I know He's Sovereign! The Gift He gave me was a gift to **"talk"**, and a <u>**hunger**</u> to research topics in order to talk about them and to express them well! He gave me a fearless desire to share my own viewpoints and to be tested under fire.

Needless to say, when you start talking confidently about <u>any</u> subject at all, people will challenge your beliefs! You better *"be ready always to give an answer to every man that asks you to give an account of the hope that lies within you".* 1 Peter 3:15.

I got "stumped" all the time in those early days, but I would go back to the research and do much better the next time that I was challenged! I got so I could represent almost any subject and debate it well. In the early days, it was usually in the political forum, since I thought that was the only way to help people. I later discovered that Political Truth is only "entry level truth". But Biblical Truth is like...WOW! It was like discovering my own Gold Mine!

I then enrolled in evening classes at the U of M and began studying Political Science. I remember an experience in my first Philosophy class. I had looked forward to that class because my heart was warming to discovering "truth". Something told me that there had to be absolutes; that life was more than the 3 tenants of the New Age which were:
 1. If it feels good...do it!
 2. If you believe it...it's true!
 3. You can't know anything for sure!

I remember discussing the last point with my cousin. I said, "If we can't know anything for sure, doesn't that disqualify itself because we are saying we "know that <u>for sure</u>"???

Anyway, I showed up at my Philosophy class, and the professor was quite late! The first day! We were all waiting in the hallway and one of the students was taking bets on illegal horse racing and I asked some of those buying them, "isn't that illegal?" They laughed and replied, "no one knows so why does it matter". I thought to myself, "so much for my discovery of truth from these guys". Then, the female professor showed up smoking those long

brown cigarettes and greeted us with some laughter and lewd words and went into the classroom where she continued to smoke. The sign above the chalk board read, "No Smoking". I think everyone was making a statement right off the bat. That is that:
1. Whatever truth is, it's not absolute, and
2. We'll respect all the personal versions of it!

I did enjoy my classes at the U of M. I learned a lot! It was easy to reject the value systems of other students because they made no sense when I tested them. My encouragement to anyone that pursues secular education is to have your value system worked out at a <u>passionate</u> and <u>studied</u> level before going there. Secular colleges have their own value systems. You'll learn the most if you let their value system role off of your soul like water off a duck's back.

The lives of John and Bob Kennedy tremendously inspired me. The deaths of them and Martin Luther King had such a profound influence that I was determined to help people. I was pursuing the doing of it in the political arena. The only one of my birthdays I do not remember at all was the one that happened the day after Bobby Kennedy was killed, June 7, 1968.

When the 1972 Presidential candidacy of George McGovern came along, I was a dedicated ideologue in his behalf. I sold my soul to getting him elected president because I thought he would change the world for the better. I had poured my life into that race believing that it would be the world's panacea! When McGovern lost, my world fell apart. It took me months to emotionally recover...seriously! Remember, I did not know Christ yet. Give me a break. I spent hours playing Spiro graph and then I would wander over to a piece of his campaign literature and mourn the loss of the election like I would mourn the loss of a loved one.

That's OK...go ahead and laugh!

I was about to experience the greatest day of my life.

Chapter Eight

The Vision in My Living Room

After the defeat of George Mc Govern for the Presidential race in 1972, a great thing happened that changed my life forever. After his failed run for the Presidency, I lost focus on everything except my resistance to the Vietnam War. I was wholeheartedly resisting the war. I not only openly resisted the Draft and campaigned against the war; I was also openly resisting paying "war taxes" and the Feds were pulling me into these conferences in the court house where I was sure I would be jailed any day. Many of my friends were going to jail, and I was ready to spend the rest of my life in jail, if need be, to make my stand.

My Brother began coming over and visiting me about his new-found faith. He began bringing others of my friends who were exhibiting these astounding life-transformations and attributing it to "getting saved". My brother was always gentle in his witness of Christ, but the others flat out told me, "Darrell, you are going to go to hell unless you get saved".

It took many visits of my brother before what he was telling me would sink in, because I thought we already were Christians. Isn't that amazing! I was doing Astral Projection, worshiping Hindu Gods and thinking I was a

Christian! We somehow believed that if our parents baptized us as a baby that that sort of "locked us in" to a rendezvous someday with heaven no matter what our own personal choices were.

Then one day in late January of 1973, it all made sense. God gave me a divine revelation of Christ on the cross. My brother had just made a simple comment on how Christ had always pursued him and if he would have just turned around from his selfish pursuits in life, he would have met Christ face-to-face years before! Tears came to his eyes. I was embarrassed in this situation for my brother's tears and turned my gaze from him to another part of the room.

Right then the greatest thing in my life happened. I saw Jesus on the cross...much bloodied. It was a vision, but I'm sure it was all in my mind. Jesus looked very much like He did in the movie "The Passion of the Christ" which I saw many years later. The vision of His cross rose to nearly the top of the 10-foot ceilings in that old South Minneapolis home. It was even bigger than life size. Christ turned His head to me, looked me directly in my eyes and said, "Darrell, I did this for you". It was like when He held out the cup of wine to His disciples at the last Supper and said, "This is my blood which was shed for you". It's personal to each one of us! I suddenly knew in my heart what my brother had been telling me when he had said, "Darrell, you need to know Christ in a personal way". At that moment I had a personal and divine revelation of Christ! In that moment, I understood that salvation was so much more than me being a nice guy. I had really been a nice guy! I patted my self on the back for it! And I loved having people tell me I was a nice guy! What arrogance to think that someday I would show up before God and wave my report card in His face and think that He would say "Olly Olly oxen free", or whatever I thought!

He alone was God's Atoning Sacrifice for my sin. This was the epitome of love defined! He took the death penalty for all the pride, misery, and sin in my life. My name was in His mind as He paid the Death Penalty for my evil! I had been trying to earn my place in life ...and maybe in heaven...by my achievements and good deeds. This gaze of His eyes into my eyes immediately pierced the vanity of all those feeble attempts. I was left naked in my soul by the revelation of how miserable was my life, and by how much He wanted me to give myself to Him like He gave Himself for me!

Unbelievably, I still fought with the Pride of my soul and did not want to surrender my life to anybody...even the living God. Those years of confusion, loneliness, and anger had hardened my heart. The days after that vision were difficult. I couldn't concentrate on my political science studies. The professors' hand was a blur as he wrote on the board. I would walk down the street and clap my heals together like on the Wrigley's gum commercials to convince myself that I was happy, but I would go home and lie in bed and tell myself, "you're a miserable, empty person".

After the vision, everything became a secondary priority to me. Christ was on my mind! The condition of my soul haunted me. Whereas before I thought I was a good man; now all I could see was my selfish motives. Up till that time I took pride in my personal character qualities, my good deeds, and my political involvement. I would even think harshly about those who never served their fellow man, or judge those who couldn't articulate political views. I would find personal solace that I understood the important things of life and was embracing those human, civil, and moral pursuits of a decent man; but now my very soul seemed to be laid bare before the white and holy light of heaven...and it was exceedingly selfish, arrogant, and sinful. For the first time, I knew my destiny was Hell unless I wholly embraced this Christ who had spoken to me and what He did for me. He Himself had personally invited me to embrace it and I knew I must surrender to Him...and I was avoiding it because I wanted to continue in a smug and self-righteous life that I could control.

During that time even Roc got saved. I thought, "him too"? He said, "Hey Joe, come here". He brought me to his upper dresser drawer and showed me a new white Bible. He told me it cost $40. and I thought, "What would make him spend $40. on a Bible???" Then he gave me about 20 of these little Gospel tracts and said, "Read these Joe". When I got home, I sat in my torn black vinyl recliner and read each one and would come to the end and read the prayer it encouraged me to pray if I was serious about becoming born again. I would moan as I read through each and never prayed that prayer.

I would intentionally set my alarm for 7AM Saturday morning so I could listen to this rather dorky Evangelist. Before that time I would mock all those radio Evangelists. I would listen to his wife, open the program with this same outdated song with her warbled voice. Tears would flow down my cheeks. I thought I was going mad, but it was the power of God and the prayers of my friends moving miraculously on my hard soul.

I remember reading a Life magazine article about the "Jesus Movement". In fact, I would read it over and over and stare at the photos of the hundreds getting baptized in the Pacific Ocean in California...and would weep...all the while stuffing more thousands of dollars under my carpet and being miserable as I would do it. Nothing satisfied.

People from my former counter counter culture were getting saved and coming over and telling me I had to get saved or face a Christ-less and hopeless eternity. I finally just started lying to them and telling them I was saved just to get them off of my back.

After a few weeks my brother asked if I wanted to go to his church. He assured me it was very different from the church that we grew up in. I asked him, "is it another hypocrite church" He assured me that it wasn't, but I had my mind made up (for no reason) that it was. As we drove up to the church I made up my mind that if one person said a derogatory comment about either George McGovern or the length of my hair that I would leave and never come back. In the church we sat way in the back in these ridiculous theater seats that were marked "for parents with small children" which made me feel even more conspicuous. This church was very different to me. Where were the towering spires, the pews, and the mysterious organ music that would come from who knows where as the congregation would sing? It was a converted funeral chapel. The robes that the choir was wearing had stains on the armpits, and the choir members were either overweight or very skinny. I began to imagine that this whole religious operation was something that had been infiltrated or created by communists. I was determined to fold my arms, wrinkle my brow and cast a gaze on everyone whose eyes met mine to let them know that I was wise to their plot to sap the strength of American youth.

To say I was confused would be an understatement! Maybe I was even losing my mind!

I was also confused because even though I saw many "Nixon for president" bumper stickers on the cars in front of the church left over from the last election, no one made political statements, nor did they fault me for my long hair, and instead greeted me very lovingly. Were these ultra Conservatives or Communists or some strange mutant mix of the two?

As they sang and as the Pastor preached, the power of God fell heavily over my soul and over-rode my strange reasoning's. I knew that I must respond to this God who was more real and more powerfully involved with people than I ever imagined. Then this very old man stood up and spoke in a foreign language right in the middle of the service. Then someone stood up and very boldly declared words that seemed from God Himself. At the end, the pastor invited people to come to the front of the sanctuary and be prayed for by him if they wanted to surrender their lives to Christ. I wanted to go do that so badly, but my pride held me back again. As he prayed with those who went up, I desired to experience the very love of God that seemed to be up there, but I remained in my pride and self-sufficiency...and misery.

After the service when we were returning home, I asked my brother what the foreign languages were all about! He explained them as "tongues" and "interpretations from God" He showed me in 1 Corinthians 12 and 14 where it spoke about this. I spent hours in my dining room that night pouring over those scriptures trying to prove that they didn't say what it seemed like they did.

You see, I did not want to be responsible to anyone but me! But yet, I also wanted to be happy!...an impossible marriage. I was about to discover Jesus words, *"he who seeks to gain his life will lose it, but he who loses his life for my sake and the Gospels, the same shall save it".*

I retired to bed and tossed and turned as I considered how wretched and confused my soul was.

Finally I rose and knelt by the foot of my bed. My battle with God was finally coming to an end, and I prayed and surrendered my all to Christ. I remembered that I prayed three things:
1) Lord let me have the relationship with Christ like my brother has,
2) God forgive my evil deeds and selfish motives, and
3) I give you my life.

That final one was the hardest one. I didn't want to give my life to anyone. After the misery I faced in school with bullies, and with the demeaning words of my step-dad year after year, I didn't want to relinquish control of my life to anyone! I didn't even like getting Novocain at the Dentist! Somehow even that represented a lack of me controlling my own life. But then I did surrender to Christ! I gave Him my whole life! I was Born Again. I arose with my soul cleansed and bathed in the bliss and divine assurance of Christ's' acceptance of me. Christ had saved me!

I gave my whole life to Christ. He overwhelmed me with His love and goodness. I was so in love with Him, that I would have gone and been a mercenary for Him anywhere.

That love lasts to this day.

JESUS INTRODUCES ME

After I surrendered to Jesus, the most wonderful thing happened. He took my hand and said, "I have someone else you need to meet", and He led me to meet my Heavenly Father! My Father in Heaven embraced me and over the years, would teach me gentleness, strength, courage, and all these manly things on how to be a man, be a dad, be a husband, and be a leader. He undid all the pain, brokenness and confusion of my childhood. He showed me about His love for Jesus His Son and how He poured out on Him all the wrath and judgment for <u>my</u> evil deeds. I wept, and loved Him even more greatly. <u>As I grew in my understanding of His great love for His Son, I understood His love for Mankind.</u> That He would give His Son to liberate us from this life-dominating curse of sin and selfishness and all of its related destruction made me understand real Celestial Love for mankind. Finally everything made sense! Life on earth, why god allows evil, human choice, destiny, freedom, Human design, and the Heart of God all made sense! This understanding of His Love is what I waited for so long, and now I have It! It is still what drives me to bring this knowledge of His Redemption to as many as possible before my life on earth runs out. The "Gospel" means "Good News"! It's the Best News!

Six months after Christ took my heart, He led me to even another wonderful relationship! It just keeps getting better! I was praying in the church prayer room and just repeating the words "Give me everything you have God, I want all you have for me" and suddenly I began to speak in another language. Although I felt a great presence of God in my life, I stopped myself. I thought it was wrong. This event was repeated in almost exactly the same way one week later. Then a few weeks later, an Evangelist was speaking at our church, and he spoke something that I believe were the very words of God to set me free. He said, "some of you speak in tongues already, and you are stopping yourself, God wants you to just let it out because it's something He gave you...it's His gift" I went to the front of the church and just began to pray in tongues quietly to myself...what a freedom was mine! Oh, what a wonderful gift and what a wonderful God!

This relationship with the Holy Spirit is for all believers! The Bible calls it a promise and He specifically says it's for you. *"The Promise is for you, your children, and to those who are afar off, even to as many as the Lord thy God shall call"* Acts 2:39. This power is promised to us in Acts 1:8 and it equips us to do our primary job which is to share our personal story (our witness) with those who are not saved. Then the Gospel *"becomes the Power of God to all who believe".* The Bible says to be continually filled with the Holy Spirit in Ephesians 5:8. Do you need to be filled right now? Ask Jesus to fill you! John the Baptist said that *"There is One Who comes after me whose sandal I'm not worthy to stoop down and unloose, He will baptize you with the Holy Spirit and with fire".* Have you received that fire?

Stop right now and ask Jesus to introduce you to all the Power of the Holy Spirit. Tell Him you want everything He has for you; and after you get it, realize that it is a promise to your children as well. If you have kids, pray right now that they will know this wonderful Baptism in the Holy Spirit and Fire!

A week later the pastor asked if I wanted to get baptized in water. I told him I was baptized with a dab of water on the head when I was a baby and maybe I should wait. He invited me to a class that he insisted was a "no-pressure class". The things he spoke of at that class were so undeniably rooted in scripture that I was baptized that very night. I felt cleansed, freed, empowered by the Almighty Himself. This was my own personal love response to Jesus. Unlike when I was a baby and my parents had my head wetted, <u>this was **my** decision, this was **my** Savior I was declaring, this was **my** experience I was giving testimony to, this was where the Sacrament of Baptism became **my own** very special & personal place of receiving Grace!</u> I gave my testimony to those observing my baptism. As I stood outside the church later, I felt so wonderful, so clean, and so free. I wish I had a photo of my smile to show you.

Have you been baptized by immersion in water? It is the Primary Sacrament of God along with Communion. The reason you need to be baptized by immersion is because it is the only way that Baptism is ever mentioned in the Bible; in fact, the very meaning of the word means to "plunge under". So then, Immersion it is!

Also, <u>Baptism always follows your conversion</u>; and it never precedes it. If you have not been baptized since Christ saved you, I believe it's time!

Baptism never saves you. Beware of any belief that implies that <u>any</u> act, ritual, or sacrament can save us. No ritual, even sacred ones like baptism and communion can save us, but they are wonderful precious love responses to the One who has!

We remember the precious Blood and Body of Christ in Communion and we follow Jesus in Water Baptism. Baptism is your own personal love response to God for the wonderful work of salvation inside you. It's not your parent's choice or your pastor's choice. It's <u>your own</u> personal choice. If your relatives can come when you get baptized, invite them, but their schedule cannot dictate your obedience! So, don't delay your baptism unduly to satisfy their schedule. And especially, don't ever let anyone else's attitudes, opinions, or design for your life, interfere with your love for Jesus. *"He who loves father or mother more than me is not worthy of me"*-Jesus

Another wonderful thing is to have a wonderful pastor. Mine was Pastor David Jones. He cared for me. He never condemned me. Even though I had long hair, and was young in the Lord, he released me into leadership with the youth. Years later I asked him how he could have trusted me. He said, "Darrell, you loved the Word. That was evident. I knew you would inspire them to love the Word too". He knew that he could always reason with me on the basis of the Bible's content and so he felt safe with me. He knew that I was teachable and would not place my own flesh or identity above my love for God's Word. He also recognized that I was an Evangelist and was not intimidated by me. He groomed me, accepted me, and taught me how to shepherd the family of God. I learned I must never condemn the people of God. I must practice patience with those who don't really aspire to excellence in their spiritual walk.

Even though there are many who do not aspire to excellence in their walk with Christ, I learned that I needed to! I had to be "wholehearted" like Joshua and Caleb and not like those who would return to the people of God with faithless reports and doubtful aspirations. I learned that I needed to hang with those who are faithful in the same way. David said, *"My eyes will be on the faithful of the land and with them will I dwell"*. Paul told his spiritual son Timothy to *"commit the things that he'd learned to faithful men who will go and do likewise"*. We bear the most precious message and the most helpful teaching that exists this side of heaven! Paul said, *"We must discharge the trust that has been committed to us"*. 1 Corinthians 9

Freedom starts in a moment and grows for a life-time.

Freedom can start in your life right now! Are you ready for a miracle?

Open your heart to everything God has for you!

The greatest law in the Bible is called by its Hebrew name-"the Shema", which simply means "hear". It's in the box below. I invite you to "hear" this greatest law under the Sun. Your surrender to it is more important than past behavior, failure, or pain. It is more important than present behavior, good works, or religious deeds. <u>In fact, the Christian life is more about surrender than it is about behavior!</u> Surrender is the secret ingredient to good behavior! Chew on that one a while! But stop now and Meditate on the 'Great Commandment". If this commandment is more than nice sounding religious words and if it is something that will guide our lives into our destiny, we must surrender to it!

> *"Thou shalt love the Lord thy God with all thy heart, and with all thy soul, and with thy entire mind, and with all thy strength, this is the first and the greatest commandment" Mark 12:30*

Chapter Nine

Converting the Den of Iniquity

Place: 4715 Pillsbury (Basement) Minneapolis, Minnesota USA
Dates: 1970-1974
Event: The Den of Iniquity
Activities: Drugs of all kinds, sale of drugs, kegs, liquor, fornication, aimlessness, laziness, arrogance, passing of gas, much TV watching, swearing, mooching food, idle chatter, idol worship, and the like
Layout: Large central basement room with chairs in a circle that facilitated passing a joint and with a keg in the middle. There were many small rooms to the side and behind that virtually consisted of a bed with a curtain on a drawstring for privacy. These were for sleeping, passing out and sometimes used for even less noble things.

My cousin Bill became a part of this group. It was his parents' house. It's where he and I had spent much of our "54 Buick" time in previous years. In fact, some of our old counter culture had become part of this group. "Roc" and I had gone our own separate ways by this time because our values had changed. He began stealing and involving himself in other selfish behavior that didn't appeal to me. Many other characters allied themselves with this group over the years and it grew to 30-40 infidels (said lovingly). The group included:

"Roc"-my cousin Bill
"Floy"-my cousin George
"Roy"-my brother Ted
"X"-The guy who we couldn't remember his name
"Mushroom"- a Vietnam vet who was unusually heavy on the top
"Fat Slob"- he didn't like this name...duh on our part?
"Gligor"- Bill's half cousin, Steve
"Krumery"-another Vietnam vet
"Dickey"-Bill's brother
"Tim Holmes"-Tim Holmes (1st and last name always pronounced together)

I did not frequent the group because I never believed in drugs. I would try to get them into Eastern Religions and they would try to get me into dope. Neither were successful, although I would go to rock concerts with them, and visit from time to time.

Understand, this chapter predates and then transitions my own salvation outlined in the previous chapter. In fact, it was Christ's power that eventually swept through the group, and that brought the group to an end. They virtually all got saved! Once their lives got straightened out, most got married. A number went into full-time ministry. Just a few, *"like a dog returning to his vomit"* went back to their old lifestyle. Surely *"the way of the transgressor is hard"*. Few of those who walked away from Christ ever got married and to this day they live a very sad & lonely life. My prayer is that they will return to the God who always loved them, and abandon their perilous ways before its completely too late.

TIM HOLMES
The key trigger in the salvation of the members of the Den of Iniquity was that God chose the worst one among

us to get saved first. His name was Tim Holmes. He was always looking for a new high. Every time we would see him he would have a new pill, a new drug, a new source for drugs, a new "head" book, some new insight, or some new philosophy or idea he would try to share with us. He made a science out of it all. Various cocktails of drugs was the pilgrimage he lived. When others in the Den would see him driving up or coming down the stairs, they would laugh and talk about how drugged he was. This from people who were drugged-constantly! I remember once he came down the ally in his red 53 Chevy convertible and called us over to him. He showed us his transparent pill box with a couple new occupants in it. He said, "this blue one is_____, and it does_____, and the brown one I do right after _____ and it does_____, and check out this book, it's called Psycho Cybernetics blah, blah. He drove away with all or us laughing. He even carried a pocket New Testament that he would pull out (before he was saved!) and as he would smoke dope, pop a pill, or drink he would read us a miracle of Jesus or something and go, "whoa, check this out! Is this cool or what! Jesus healed the blind man! Wouldn't it be cool to see that?"

My Brother did so many drugs that he couldn't even cut his side-burns straight. White stuff was always coming out of the sides of his mouth. He would always speak with slurred words. Sometimes when he slept, we thought he was dead! My Grandmother would weep bitter tears. The guy was absolutely lost! You can see how it stirred my heart when he and Tim Holmes showed up at my house in perfect shape to share with me what Jesus had done in their lives!

The great change in the Den of Iniquity began one evening when Tim Holmes was at home smoking dope and doing other intoxicants while watching Billy Graham. He was intrigued by the words and especially the altar call.

"Why are all those people walking up to the stage? What is it doing to them?" he asked himself. He went for a walk to clear his mind. He came to a place on Nicollet and Diamond Lake Road called **"His Place"**. Just a little store front with a silhouette of Jesus on the front window with that name over it. He thought to himself, "This is what Billy Graham was talking about". He went in! Inside there were two volunteers: Norm Norland and Ethyl Mahoney. The former was a no nonsense right-to-the-point Christian. The latter had the softest and most caring heart in the world. As Tim walked in and began asking questions about God, it was obvious that he was stoned. Ethyl comforted him and poured out her heart to him about Christ's love. Norm thought to himself, "This is a mockery of God's love" and ordered Tim that if he was sincere about his search for God that he must drop to his knees and appeal to God with cries of repentance and plead for God's mercy in a loud voice. To his and Ethyl's amazement, he did it! Tim was born again and forever changed.

The next day, Tim Holmes showed up at the Den of Iniquity and took his normal seat in the circle as a joint was being passed around. When the joint came to him, he held it at arms length and said, "This is dumb". Listen to the extensive vocabulary that ensued:

My cousin George responded, "no it's not".
Tim responded, "Yeah it is"
George: "it's not dumb, it's neat"
Tim Holmes: "no, the Lord is neat!"
George: "they're both neat"
Tim Holmes: "nope, the Lord is neat and this is dumb"

Tim passed the joint on, got up and walked out of the room.

That value judgment started a ball rolling that is still rolling today. Tens of thousands have come to Christ through our ministries since then and it all began with that decision!

My Brother was sitting in his favorite easy chair right by the stairs. He was stoned as usual and with his muddled brain he thought to himself, "What happened to Tim?" Little did he know that in a few days he would find a Gospel tract in a phone booth and pray the prayer at the end of it? Now two were saved! They talked with others. More were born again. Dope and liquor were flushed down the toilet. They would brainstorm on who wasn't saved and then go to them and they would come to Christ. I was one of them.

We all began living a life of being a witness for Jesus! Doing the great things like winning others to Jesus and prison and hospital ministry. My brother and I led both of our grandparents to Christ on their deathbeds. My Stepdad's Dad had led an angry and cruel life. He cried out to God on his deathbed in his own words, "Lord forgive me for my many sins and iniquities" He died in the arms of Jesus. We prayed for a family friend who had been pistol whipped and was in a permanent vegetative state. He suddenly "woke up". It scared the nurse so much that she dropped her tray! Nursing home residents would sob and surrender to Christ as the Spirit of God would move through the room. I led my aunt to Christ as she lay completely paralyzed from a brain aneurism. I wasn't even sure she could hear me and then tears began flowing from her eyes and down her nose as we prayed. Her son, my cousin came to Christ 12 hours before he died. He called me and asked me to visit him. I almost said I was too busy, but instead I went, and he surrendered to Christ!

Christian Ministry flows from the believer like water flows from a faucet. Ephesians 2:10 says, *We are God's workmanship in Christ Jesus, created to do good works which God has before ordained that we should walk in them"*

I must give thanks to one man. Pastor David Jones who had the vision to start the Coffee House and who became our Pastor. His church was filled with converted Hippies. Some Parishioners were aghast as barefoot Hippy types stuck gum under the seats and would give the most audacious "prophetic words from God". To be sure, and to their credit, most were patient with us. With Pastor Jones leadership they became a family to us. Rev. Jones is the only one I have called "Pastor" throughout all of my spiritual life. He presided at my marriage to Ellie and the dedication of our first two kids. I owe him my life. He taught me to love the Word as I mentioned previously

Today many shrink away from public ministry. It indeed is one of the great privileges of life. Paul exhorted his spiritual son Timothy, *"preach the Word, be ready in season and out, let no man despise your youth but be an example in speech, in life, in love, in faith, and in purity...give yourself to the public reading of scripture".* Learning how to express ideas with clarity and passion is one of the most fulfilling things to do while on this planet. And others need it! You are a living letter that others need to read. Study the Word, then go and share its life giving revelation to every audience and individual you can find. You have the very words of God!

Maybe one of those individuals you share with will be the next Tim Holmes or someone in your next audience will bring revival to the next Den of Iniquity.

I'll close this chapter with one of the most important things I've ever learned:

Christians need Christian friends!

We literally become part of one another's life, zeal, courage, growth, healing, revelation, and joy! The biblical word for fellowship in the original biblical language is the word "Koinonia". It means to "have a participative sharing in one another's life! In fact, the phrase "one another" occurs scores of times in the Bible and refers to over 50 areas that we are to have this "participative sharing"! i.e.
        love one another
        pray for one another
        forgive one another
        instruct one-another
        exhort one another
        bear one another's burdens
        encourage one another
        serve one another
        stimulate one another to love and good deeds
        And on and on!

What happened in the conversion of the "Den of Iniquity" is the ideal situation and it is what we need always reach for in winning the lost. We must stand for Christ with our Witness. Minister the Gospel in power and see men converted. You must decide if you will be a Disciple of the Lord Jesus Christ or if you're going to be just a Believer. Bowing over in weakness to our old ways, and hanging with people who endlessly make excuses about what they can not do is not the way of a Disciple.

Know this for sure! You will be hit, you will be slammed, and you will be shamed. Its not easy living the life of a disciple! But they are the only ones who will leave their mark on this globe for the glory of Jesus!

There is a "synergy" that takes place among passionate people! One plus one no longer equals two. It equals four or ten or a hundred or a thousand! As you hang around and work with passionate Christian disciples, you will be amazed at what you will accomplish! You will catch yourself performing beyond what you ever thought possible! It's the power of Christian fellowship! It's the power of Koinonia! The "normal" Christian life is one of passionate, confident, courageous Christian expression and friendship! The farther we can separate ourselves from those who just want to be believers, the better.

If you're in a dead church right now, the best thing you can get out of it is yourself!

Get out! Find a passionate people to be with. King David said, *"My eyes will be on the faithful of the land, and with him will I dwell".* Where are you eyes today? Are you living with faithful people?

> **God has not given us a spirit of timidity, but of power, of love, and of self control. So do not be ashamed of the testimony of our Lord..." 2 Timothy 1:7, 8**

Chapter Ten

Brown Hair and a Bandanna

I'd never seen anything so beautiful! I was trying to control myself from not staring! She was wearing a Bandanna. She might as well have been wearing a thief's mask because she was about ready to steal my heart.

She walked in with Sue Easton, a gal who had been saved in our Coffee House and attended our Bible Study for a few months. They both worked on the U of M campus. They had met waiting for an elevator that was stuck. After a long delay, the group of disgruntled people waiting for the elevator began to murmur their complaints to one another. Sue broke the mood with an "Oh well, praise the Lord". Ellie asked Sue, "Are you a Christian?" They got to know each other, and Sue let her know that there was this great group of young people meeting for Bible Study. The next thing you know, Ellie is walking through the door with that Bandana wrapped around the most beautiful brown hair you ever saw. We'll talk of the brown eyes later!

Week after week she attended. I had never been attracted to anyone this way before! I had had some try to be a girlfriend to me, but I wasn't interested. Whoa dude, this one was different!

Every Tuesday night I looked forward to seeing her at Bible Study. Womanizing was not exactly my cup of tea. All the other guys would talk to her and I couldn't compete, right? I mean, I had spent years with no friends at all. How could I compete for such a woman? I was tempted to retreat back into my shyness and fear, but...well, let me endeavor to replay my thoughts that I had over the weeks as I wanted to get up the courage to begin a relationship:

"What would she see in me anyway? I'm not that cool of a guy."

"Oh, well, I'll just give up. Yes! Christ is enough for me anyway!"

"Hmmm, it's not working; I still want to get to know her."

"Ok, time for a strategy. As soon as we say amen after prayer at Bible study I need to make my move. Let's see, I'll assess my position...Bill Snow is next to me...he always goes right up and talks to her. I'll have to get up quickly to beat him and the others, but I can't be too conspicuous."

So I applied the Strategy, and it worked! I got up quickly after the "Amen" and beat the other guys to her. Walla! I was talking to her. Me! I was talking to her!

My heart quickly got wrapped up in this girl. I invited her to a Christian-Christmas play at the Chanhassen Dinner Theater. I remember seeing her across from me, and looking in her eyes, suddenly fear struck me. I thought, "what if she's like only 17 or even 18?" I was almost afraid to ask! When she said she was 21 it was a huge relief. I then became aware of how classy she was compared to me. She was ravishing! I had on this unearthly combination of clothes out of my past...yes, my old Monkee clothes. I couldn't help it. It was the closest thing to dress up clothes I had. She didn't seem to mind a

110

bit and even seemed to enjoy my company! Imagine that! A girl enjoying my company???

But Christ's love is always a jealous love and His Spirit is always purifying it in our hearts. Ellie's place began to encroach on Christ's place. God always whispers some words in our ear when some other Love begins setting up a rival throne. It happened to me two times: The first time was when I was headed to Bible study on Tuesday night a few months after the Dinner Theater thing. I was singing and happy as I was driving there after work. Into that seemingly joyous place, God spoke to me. "Why are you going to Bible Study?" I replied, "To study the Bible". The Lord responded, "No, you're going to see Ellen". I said, "God can't I have just one private spot in my life?" But He was right; I repented and renewed my love for Him, and was much happier because of it. I was even much more able to be free and confident in my relationship with Ellen when I didn't "need" her to rule my emotions from a rival throne in my heart. Love Christ supremely. Sharing your love with someone else always seems to come back and bite us

The other time when God tested me was when Ellie reacted to me always inviting her to hear preachers rather than invite her out on a "real date". I realized from that point that I must level with her about where my heart was at. I had to explain to her that my heart belonged totally to Christ's and that I would be involved in Christian Ministry my whole life. I brought her for a ride in my 57 Chrysler (I bought this one after the first one got wrecked). I told her where my heart was and then told her she was playing her guitar for the wrong motive and she must love Christ supremely. I said, "Why are you playing your guitar in secular coffeehouses?" She replied, "I do it for Ministry". I then said, "No you're not, you're doing it to show off". BIG MISTAKE! Let me teach you all something right here:

DON'T QUESTION PEOPLES MOTIVES-**EVER!** Whether in Leadership, Ministry, or Marriage, don't question people's motives! It gets you in hot water that you can't get out of.

She got very angry and asked to be brought home. I dropped her off, but noticed she left her Sweater in the back seat. Ah ha! This was my ticket to seeing her again! What am I saying!!! I decided to not call her again. I again committed my life to the study of scripture and to Christian Ministry. But then, a phone call. Ellie calls me and invites me to a back yard Barbeque. Part of me went "yes!", and part of me went, "Oh no." So I went and gave her Sweater back and enjoyed the barbeque and took her for a ride where I clarified again what it means to serve God with all of your heart. She was again bothered, but this time not angry.

The next day I get a knock on the door. It's Ellie in tears. She explained about how she went down to the lake where we had talked the day before to think about all I had said to her. Some young men approached her to invite her to a party and made suggestive comments. She got up and left them and came to my place and said, "Darrell, you're the only one I feel safe around" What a complement!

The relationship developed rapidly from that point. I was completing a Ministry degree at NCU and we were married in the middle of my training. August 7, 1976. For our Honeymoon we drove around Lake Superior in my 57 Chrysler. We got numerous comments, "are you guys just married?" We'd asked them how they knew. They said it was written all over us.

That was 40 years, 5 kids, and 13 grandkids ago. Memories of life with Ellen are like a wondrous harbor that I visit often. She was the most fun and faithful wife a man could ask for. She had this nobility that I think her

English Dad instilled in her. She brought identity and a purifying freshness to my home. Yes, she moved into the house I grew up in. All the darkness of my lost years was swept away as her presence created this new Identity to everything. As she would bake bread, care for our children, put her sprouts in the window, or sit in her stripped pajamas cross legged on the bed with her Guitar composing new songs, my life finally was rescued from the past. I had found a brand new joyous identity with this brown-eyed beautiful smiling dream of my Life whose name means... "Radiant one".

Then and now, she has always loved the Word. She still fights the fight of faith with persistence to overcome the things that would try to hold her or her family down. She was the first in her troubled family to be saved and she began a legacy in her family line which will endure a thousand generations.

She has been my Helper, my Prayer Warrior, my Prayer Partner, my Defender, my Worship Leader, My Credibility Giver, my Encourager, my Office Assistant, my Broadcast Partner, my Book Editor, a fantastic Home Maker and Cook, and who knows what all I missed. Oh yeah, she's done her share of Bus Cleaning & Diaper Changing too!

> *"He who finds a wife finds a good thing and obtains favor from the Lord" Proverbs 18:22*

Chapter Eleven

Minnesota's Most Prominent Homosexual

"Wow! That's beautiful!" The sound of concert piano music again came from the house next door. Bruce Brockway was the tenant and he was a professional Concert Pianist. He often played at the Guthrie Theater. He was rich, talented, tremendously good looking, wore great clothes, had lots of cultured friends…and he was Gay.

He was actually the first guy to die of AIDS in Minnesota! He was also editor of the state gay newspaper

In my early Christian years, I had the greatest problem building bridges to two kinds of people, rich people and Gay men. Bruce Brockway was both.

God began speaking to my heart that Bruce was like a sheep without a Shepherd. I told God, "Well, that's fine that you feel like that God, but don't send me to him! Why would he want to talk to me anyway? He's cultured and I'm not! Please God, send someone else." He had lots of visitors, nearly all men, and I fought being one. I'll visit other people, I told myself, but not Bruce Brockway.

How many of you know that God always wins an Argument?

PURSUING A NEW HABIT -Another Humorous story

At that same time in my life, I was trying to develop the habit of rising early to seek the Lord. I felt like God wanted me to rise at 4:30 AM and seek His face and study His Word. The problem is, I had never learned the discipline of going to bed early! You've got the Arithmetic working against you if you go to bed at 11PM or Midnight and then try to get up at 4:30!

I tried everything. My first efforts were with my clock radio. It would go off at 4:30 and I would just shut it off and go back to sleep. I went out and bought one of those Big-Ben wind-up alarm clocks because they had a louder bell. It had this little push-in thing on the back to shut the alarm off. So, when morning came, I just pushed in the little shut off thing and went back to bed. I then got the idea to wind masking tape around the little push-in thing so I couldn't push it in. It went off and I tried to shut it off, but I couldn't push the post thing in. I pushed as hard as I could. Finally, in frustrated anger, I threw it against the wall and it sort of went ding, ding,,,,,ding,,,,,,,,,faintly ding; and then died.

The problem with this whole picture is that I lived right next door to Bruce Brockway and our Bedroom windows were right across from each other and in the summer months we both kept our windows open; so my struggle to be more godly was like an open book that I was forcing him to read at 4:30 each morning!

Well, I finally figured out the failsafe plan to get my unspiritual and tired body out of bed at 4:30. I went out to

Radio Shack and bought one of those things that turns lights on and off at preset times to scare away Burglars. I plugged my Phonograph Turntable into it (back then we used vinyl records to listen to music). I had a record by a very passionate musician named Keith Green. One of the songs on it was called "Altar Call" and one of the lines in the song goes "*...but you, you can't even get out of bed*". I thought that I could maybe condemn myself out of my spiritual lethargy! I set the contraption for 4:30; I queued up the Record to the above Phrase, I turned the knob to channel the music through the bedroom speakers when it went off, and cranked the volume up to 10-**the max**.

Well the bomb was set, the fuse was lit, and it was going to explode at 4:30. It went off like an atomic explosion! I was so jolted and so disoriented that I did not know which way was up. All I could think of is that I've got to get to the living room and turn it off. I stumbled rapidly out of my bed. Then over the sound of this earthquake I hear a very loud voice of Bruce Brockway shouting from his next-door Bedroom window, "Turn the d__ thing off". I got it off and then I paced the floor for the next 2 hours asking God to forgive me for being such a bad witness...but, finally, I was talking to God at 4:30 in the morning!

I DID IT!

You know, I got the discipline worked out where I didn't need Keith Green anymore!

For the next 10 years I rose at 4:30AM and talked to God before I started the day. I wrestled with Demons; I walked with God; Gods Word opened up new vistas of truth and revelation to me. It was like I would walk out from the very Presence of God and interface with the

World in a Heavenly way! Every day, God gave me specific ideas and direction; Jesus even came and appeared to me once. I thought I was going mad, but it was Him. His face was like a flame of fire! I looked right into it! He said, "Darrell, things will become so difficult in the work I've called you to that you will want to give up, only don't give up". He then revealed specific things to me that were fulfilled to the "T" over the next years. Up until that point I had had very little difficulty in ministry, but soon after this word from God, I had many difficult times that would have caused me to give up had it not been for this appearance of Jesus to me. It is one of the most profound things that ever happened. I rarely share it because people would think me mad. It is difficult to share it without tears.

Be very aware my fellow Pilgrim that you can be experiencing immense growth and be having problems at the same time!

In the midst of the problems, God says these promises to all of us:

"I will be with you always until the end of the age"

"I am a rewarded of those that diligently seek me."

"I am He who knows you and I will make your ways prosper"

"When you walk through the fire, it will not burn you and when you walk through the ocean, it will not drown you".

"If I am for you, who is he who condemns you; who can come against you"

"I will order the steps of a good man". And remember, a good man is not defined as someone who is perfect, but someone who is surrendered!

God is with you! His Paternity over you did not come by you growing up in the right place or being a nice guy! He said, "You have not chosen me, but I have chosen you and ordained you to bring forth much fruit". He said, "To as many as received Him, to them gave he the right to be sons of God"! You are God's son. You will overcome every obstacle. You will succeed.

OK, before I finish my story about Bruce Brockway, I've got to share one of the most hilarious things that have ever happened in my life! My sister and future husband (Don Lawson, -a guy who got saved at my work) scheduled a date to get married. I lived in a Duplex and they were scheduled to be married in three days and were planning to move into that Apartment. The problem is that it had all hardwood flooring that had been painted with grey paint and they wanted to restore them before moving in. Well, sanding 4 full rooms takes a day of hard work. Then you have to put on at least 2 coats of Varnish that take a day each to dry. The Arithmetic was working against us. We could do it, but we would have to stay up all night sanding floors.

If you have seen Floor Refinishing, you know that it is a very noisy operation. There is a main sander called a "Drum Sander". This is like the most powerful Sander known to man! You have to be careful you don't let the thing sit in one place even for a moment or it will put a huge divot in your floor. It's powerful. The rental store gave us this 24 grit sandpaper wrap around the disk to use to get up the grey deck paint. Let this amateur embellish the story a bit!!! It's like a big strong sheet of paper with 10 rocks glued to it. If you left it in one place it would cut a hole all the way through the floor & probably dig its way into the Basement. We had to unplug every Appliance in the house to keep it from blowing the main fuse. We even unplugged Clocks. When you turn this thing on, there is so much electricity going through the power line that it actually straightens out a little. I kid you not. It pulls that much power. Then there's a thing called an Edger that you get up close to the wall with and this thing turns at about 10 million RPM and screams so loud that if you don't wear ear plugs, you'll be deaf in 5 minutes.

So, its 2 AM in the morning and Don & I are highly motivated to get this job done. We had to get the sanding done and put on the first coat of varnish so it could dry a day and while it's drying, we would sleep during the day. Then we would put on the next coat, go to bed and the next day, he would get married.

Don's running the Drum Sander and I'm running the edger. All the windows are open to get rid of the sawdust...guess who lives next door? Suddenly, I think I hear a knock on the door. I listen! Sure enough, someone's knocking really hard at 2AM in the morning. Don and I turn off our machines. Remember, mine is going 10 million RPM and takes a long time to stop. Don's has the sandpaper with the rocks glues on, and doesn't dare dig it into the floor to stop it. Both machines noise is slowly going away as the knocking gets louder. Finally I answer the back door. Guess who it is. You guessed it! Bruce Brockway standing there in the tightest purple silk briefs I've ever seen in my life. He looks me square in the eyes and just says calmly, "you've got to be kidding", and then walks down the stairs.

We did stop the work, but started again at 7AM

COURAGE ARRIVES

Well, I finally got up the courage to visit him. I knocked on his door a little sheepishly thinking he would bring up all those noisy things that had gone on in my house at 2 & 4:30 in the morning, but he didn't. He had on silk pajamas and invited me to sit down on his crushed-velvet red sofa as he sat across from me. I shared my testimony about what Jesus had done in my life. His response surprised me. He said he grew up in a Baptist church and used to go to AWANA, a great children's program where Scripture memorization is a big thing for the kids to do. He said he got married and then went to the U of M to further his music studies where he met some teachers that got him into the Gay lifestyle. He ended up divorcing his wife. It was a very sad story. He ended with, "I guess that I don't accept what the Bible says about my lifestyle and so my belief in God is different than it used to be and you probably can't convert me".

The following months I would see him working in his garden, hear the music, and see the friends, but didn't say too much.

He finally came down with full blown AIDS. Back then, AIDS victims would always get a form of cancer that was always treated with radiation. He lost his nice curly hair. His skin turned grey and you could see his bones through his skin. I went to visit him again and he told me about the progression of the Disease but had great hope that some home remedies would rescue him from it. He continued to have no interest in the Gospel. I would see him out struggling to push his Lawn Mower and wincing in pain as he would fight through his daily activities with great perseverance. He had far fewer friends visiting him now. He got an injury on his finger that would not heal. His ability to play his beloved piano was gone. I thought to myself how this is so like the Devil! He gets us to serve his desires as he deceives us and tells us it is better than the council of God, and then he destroys us and gloats as he does.

He naturally ended up in the Hospital where I had the joy of meeting his godly born-again mother. We would have talks in the hallway away from Bruce and she would tell me what a sweet and talented boy he was. He would memorize the Bible verses and skip off to the Baptist church to attend the AWANA class. She told me his dad was a drunk and an abusive man. Whenever Bruce would play the piano, he would cuff him on the head and call him a sissy. The Dad was much closer to the other two boys who turned out more like the Dad. I.e. Loud, abusive, macho, drinking types.

I never saw those well-dressed friends visit him. Maybe they did when I wasn't there.

He was in the University Hospital in Minneapolis. Years before, I used to hold "peace demonstrations" just a few blocks from where Bruce lay dying. We thought we had all the answers. I wanted to go out the doors of the hospital and just yell, "you don't know anything about peace...you don't know anything about love...come and visit this man! Where are his Lovers now? Someone help him!"

My final visit was just a few days before he died. He couldn't talk anymore because of the progression of the disease. I could tell that his mom had been in to see him before I got there because there were headphones on him that were playing concert piano music. I sat next to him on the bed and gently removed the headphones. I put a hand on his boney shoulder. He lay in a fetal position with his grey skin stretched over his bones. There was nothing left of the impressive Concert Pianist that used to wow thousands. I said, "Bruce can you hear me"? -no response. I did it again and wiggled his shoulder. "Bruce, this is your next door neighbor, Darrell. Do you know I'm here?" He nodded his head yes. I said, "Bruce, I have some words of love, can I share them with you?" He nodded his head yes.

I remembered what his mother told me about his childhood...about his abusive dad. God gave me these words for him: "Bruce, your mother told me about your childhood. It must have been so hard when your Dad treated you so harshly. And Bruce, your Heavenly Father wept with you during those times, and even though your earthly father was unfaithful, your Heavenly Father was faithful to you then and is still faithful now. He saw you skipping off to AWANA and he saw your heart; that you wanted to please Him, and he loved you. Even though your earthly father was unfaithful, your Heavenly Father has always been faithful, and He's faithful to you today! Suddenly tears started steaming down his face and he began shaking all over and weeping. He returned to Jesus just two days before he died.

You say, "How do you know since he couldn't talk"?

I know! And someday I'll introduce you to him in Heaven.

Chapter Twelve

The Voice of God!

It was another great day at work and as I drove home, I smiled at the sunshine and thought about some of the day's achievements. As I walked from my car up to my House, I was surprised to seem to have the Spirit of God speak to my heart. "Go to North Central Bible College". I walked into my front porch and knelt down on the little sofa out there. "How about the job I love?" I asked God, "I love it, and they're advancing me and even preparing me to be Vice President"? God let me know that I WAS TO RESIGN AND TRUST HIM and pursue College for Ministry preparation.

Well, I disobeyed the Lord, and for the next few months I was miserable. Finally I made the plunge, put in my resignation at my job, and became a Second-Semester entrant at North Central Bible College in January of the following year.

My great boss, Bob Strom, let me keep my former salary and hired me part time in the evening. He even informed me that the company would pay my tuition. I declined the offer to pay my tuition, but accepted the part-time evening offer.

College life was grand. I was more motivated than ever in my life and always got "A's".

A few days into my new college life, I almost got short-circuited. Back then, there were very strict guidelines one had to follow and I was not exactly a cultured or a submissive person. The dean of men hit me up in the hall about wearing jeans and that my Mustache was too long. "Not beyond the corner of the lip" he barked in a very disrespectful way. It brought back aching memories of the Principle in High School telling me not to return "until I cut my hair". I went on to my New Testament History class just seething underneath and thinking, "What kind of two-bit college is this. I'm quitting and I'm gonna get my old job back". Right then the Spirit of God spoke very clearly to me. He said, "Who called you to this College"? "You did", I replied. "So, did you decide to come to this college because they asked or did I ask you to?" I said, "Well, yeah, I came because you asked". God just said, "Then submit to its rules".

It set me free! I joyfully shaved my mustache and changed my pants. I learned a lot about how to respect Authority that I didn't agree with and to trust God to work through them even if they do things wrong.

> *"Likewise you younger people, submit yourselves to those who are over you in the Lord; and be clothed with humility for God resists the proud, but gives grace to the humble."* **Peter**

Another time I almost quit was also in my first year. One of the professors, Orel Krans, got on a harangue about Communists and political opinions about the Vietnam War which I had deep disagreements with. I was breathing hard as I said to myself, "I'm outta here. I'm not going to listen to this C___! Later that day I stormed into his office with the veins standing out in my head and said, "you have no business bringing up political opinions about the war in a Bible College class..blah..blah! He responded, "You're right Darrell. My comments were wrong. Could you find it in your heart to forgive me?'

I was caught off guard! I was prepared for a big argument and then possibly to quit the college. Truly "a soft answer turns away wrath!" I learned about the power of kindness and of humility from that man. I learned that as leaders, we don't have to always be right, and that real men don't need to defend themselves!

Rev. Krans became a spiritual father to me. After that, we would share meals, and pray. One time he was sick and I visited him in the hospital. He was the only older man other than Pastor Jones who had ever showed an interest in me. I found myself reaching for whatever grade was above an "A" in his classes so that I could be sure that I wasn't leaning on the relationship for favors. He would set me up with ministry with troubled youth. He knew that I had a story of God's deliverance in my life that could help them. Then a disaster happened. He had a heart attack and died. I went to his funeral and couldn't even go in. It was like déjà vou with my Dad when I was nine. Another dad had died of heart problems! I stayed in the foyer, listened to the service and wept. It was like a second Dad is now taken from me, and like my own Dad, in his forties. Orel's influence lives on in my life. I know his biological son, John, well. I feel like we almost had the same father.

"A TIME TOGETHER"

Two years into college, as I was driving across the Lake Street Bridge, the Spirit of God spoke to me and said, start a radio program". I said, "I don't know anything about radio" He said, "Go look around at the KNOF radio studio; you'll learn" That was the beginning of our radio program, "A Time Together", that touched thousands of lives. Many came to Christ and still love Him passionately today. They've raised their kids to be "World Changers", Christian lawyers, Pastors, church elders, and faithful Parents themselves. Some became missionaries. We linked A Time Together up with a Bible Study that we simply called "Koinonia" (Greek for "Fellowship"). We would invite people to this Bible Study. They would come with incredible problems and God met them, and we shared sweet fellowship. God saved Marriages. My wife would lead worship with her guitar and the power and love of God would engulf us.

God told us to do crazy things, and through all of them, God would save souls. We would have big "Baptism Banquets" down at Cedar Lake where dozens would get baptized. The joyous celebration of our reigning King would fill the air, and Covenant relationships between God and man would take the place of former lives of misery and pride. The church, Koinonia Assembly", grew from this fellowship.

Here's a few of the personal stories:

Ken & Pam: Pam first visited "Koinonia' with a friend named Sue. When asked to share her story, she said, "I've been listening to your radio broadcast on my way home from work for weeks. My Marriage with Ken has been under stress and now a guy at work has been making advances to me and being real sweet. I knew that if I didn't come here tonight, I would probably be in an affair tomorrow!" Wow! I thought, we sure get people confessing a lot at these Bible studies! Pam wonderfully met the freedom and forgiveness of Christ that night, and has loved and served her Rescuer & Redeemer ever since.

We began to pray for her husband, Ken. As I learned more about this man, I realized he may be a formidably difficult nut to crack! He had not wanted her to continue coming to Koinonia, and one time when she was leaving the house he continued the argument in front of the neighborhood by yelling to her as she was leaving; "go ahead, go to your little Holy Ghost, Holy Roller Bible study. The door will be locked when you get home. Well, Pam finally got him to consent to having "the preacher" and his wife over to their home for Dinner. Pam told me later that he had firmly warned her that "if that Holy Ghost Preacher comes in singing 'Glory Hallelujah' I'm going to punch him right in the nose!" You will never believe what happened! I've always loved singing. My mom lived that example for me and after I got saved, I just loved singing the old upbeat Christian camp-meeting songs. I literally walked into their house singing "Glory, Glory Hallelujah, since I laid my burdens down". I wondered why Pam looked over at Ken suddenly and he looked back with steely eyes. My nose remained intact, however thanks to Ken's pre-redemptive civility. The dinner was great: Spaghetti with a beautifully set table and wonderful hospitality. Later I had a wonderful discussion with Ken...we had a common denominator: we were both motor-heads. He

129

showed me his Roadster and we finished out a great night.

I discovered a second common denominator with Ken: Kite flying! This is an amazing testimony of the creative power of the Holy Spirit. After that night, we continued in prayer for the salvation of Ken's soul. He was firmly established in his Lutheran church where he was a Deacon. The week after our dinner at the Galls I was asking God for fun fellowship ideas for the next month. God said, "Have a kite flying day". I argued with God and said, "That's an awfully strange church event"! He assured me that I should do it, and it was scheduled. Now, Ken never came to our Church, Bible Study, or any of our events...but he showed up at this one! I asked him why he came and he said, "I love flying kites"! Wow! I had no idea, but we sat on the side of the hill with kites in our hands and talked about the glories of Christ and he surrendered his life to Christ. Only God can do things so perfect, creative, and fun!

He has been a faithful leader of his family as well as a dear friend of mine. They have supported our Missionary activity in Guatemala and India over the years. Their children embraced their parent's Christian zeal and found places of ministry and influence in the faith themselves.

The Tjaden Family: I first met Barb at my place of employ. I had hired her to run a machine that produced plastic parts. She was a talker, and had a thoroughly animated personality. A few conversations into my knowing her, it was clear she was deeply lost and so I asked the Holy Spirit for "open doors" and anointing in sharing the Savior with her. Those open doors were realized and she surrendered to the Savior. She became the "fire starter" of Salvation for her family. One by one she invited her siblings to Christ and to the "Koinonia" Bible study and the Holy Spirit was powerful in revealing the Redeemer to them. Her brother Paul, who is now one of our missionaries, had a rocky beginning. He was 17 when Barb invited him to "go to church with her". He thought it was the large Lutheran church where the family would attend upon occasion. When they pulled up in front of the converted funeral home (now a Church) where I was a youth leader, he began an argument with her. "What's this?" He shouted. She hushed him enough and bought his confidence enough for just that one visit. They came into my teen Sunday school class where he took issue with my statement of knowing for sure we can go to heaven. The need to surrender to the Savior gripped his soul. He prayed right there. He says it was one week later that it really "stuck" when he prayed again. He is a Covenant Brother of mine to this day.

Their sister Diane got saved, and one by one the other kids did too and finally just a few years ago, the oldest brother Marty gave his life to Christ. It took hundreds of prayers and many years but now the whole family is in the Kingdom...and it all started with a conversation and a commitment to Jesus at a Plastics Factory

Recently, their mom, Dorothy died, and I had the privilege of doing the funeral for the family. Dorothy had surrendered to Christ after surrendering her proud personal ways to the Cross. She found peace in her service to the Savior and even accompanied me to Mexico with a group from her church. I knew how "converted" she was when we had to sleep Dorm style on the floor of a Mexico chicken farm! When I saw this formerly very self involved woman carry out her responsibilities at her church and now with peace and humility in outreach ministry, it was a joyous example of the great work Christ had done in her.

Don & Cheryl: My first acquaintance with Don is when I was training him to be a "Set-up Man" at our plastics firm. To say he was rough around the edges and misguided with life would be like saying the Grand Canyon is a pretty big hole. I loved his jokes though! We would sit around on our lunch break and he would tell me the wildest jokes; & stories about his past (and present). I honestly enjoyed my relationship with this lost soul.

I would intercede before God for this man for months as I shared the Gospel with him seemingly to no avail. Then one day, he notified me he was leaving and moving to California. I thought his soul would maybe be lost forever, but wholly committed him to God's care and assured him I would pray for him as he left. To my surprise, he shows up at our doorstep one year later asking for his job back. I said, "Hey Don, What did you do in California?" "I'll tell you about it later". And boy did he ever! He could write a book on the colorful, but sordid experiences of those days.

My intercession for him and the Holy Spirits' intervention continued powerfully in his life. There were many times he would almost be jailed, killed, or hurt and I spoke to him words of warning. One time he spoke to me about narrowly missing disaster the night before with a wheel coming off of his car and I said, "Don, you know the truth of Christ and you are rejecting it. The Bible says, *'he that is often reproved and hardeneth his neck shall suddenly be cut off and then without mercy'*. You need to get right with God!"

Not long after, I saw Don by the door during shift change when all the Foremen, Setup Men, and Machine Assistants were together for our daily transfer of shift information. Up until this day, Don was their drinking and dope smoking buddy. The Spirit of God whispered to my heart, "Don gave his life to me". I boldly blurted out. "Don, did you get saved last night?" One of the guys said, "Yeah, Lawson got saved, ha, ha, ha." Others chuckled. Don said nothing. In surprisingly great confidence I said, "You know Don, Jesus said that if we deny Him before men, He will deny us before our Father in Heaven. If you got saved, you better admit it". He replied, "Yeah I did"...you could hear a pin drop.

That began a wonderful era of relationship with this genuine man and covenant brother who shortly after his conversion married my sister, Cheryl!!! She had gotten saved about the same time and began going to my Church. They became missionaries to Amsterdam until their 6th kid was born. Now they have 12 kids who all love Jesus. You can't make this stuff up!

My sister is an outspoken proclaimer of what she calls Biblical Womanhood, and is one of the most enduring and joyful people I know. She is also my greatest Ally and friend in all the family issues. Don completely abandoned his previous life by God's grace and raised his 12 children being an impeccable example of fidelity and faithfulness to His God and family.

Pam & Kent: Not to be confused with Pam and Ken! Pam showed up at Koinonia, invited by a friend. She quickly surrendered all to Christ and found freedom in her soul. Her husband would threaten her every time she went to Bible Study. One time he tersely warned her, "If you go to that group tonight, when you come home tonight, I'm going to wait until you're asleep and then I'm going to cut out your intestines with a knife, and show them to you as you die". We all prayed, "Oh Lord, protect Pam from this horrible plan". The next week Pam shows up greeting everyone with a smile, followed by this very tall man. We all thought, "Is this the guy that was going to cut out her intestines?" He sat quietly during the entire study, and at the very end while we were standing in a circle getting ready to pray, he said, "Hey, do you suppose I could give my life to Christ?"

Oh Yeah!

They serve Christ to this day. Kent also mentored me in rebuilding Bus Motors when I began running coaches into Mexico for Mission Work.

Steve Treberg: He was a frequent listener to a "A Time Together" radio broadcast. He was shacking up and living an immoral life and finally he called and we talked and he surrendered to Christ. He became a faithful attendee of "Koinonia", helped with everything, and became a missionary at our YWAM missionary base in Arkansas. We've worked together on the streets of Minneapolis, Mexico, and

Guatemala. We've broken bread and paddled together in the BWCA. Finally after many years, he married a wonderful friend, Renee and they have three kids

Bob & Elinor: These are my parents! Remember the relationship I had with my dad? The transitional day was when I was visiting my mom and my dad returned early. I was in the kitchen and I heard him come in the front door. Now, during my visits to my mom, I would always leave before my dad returned from work. This day he had gotten off early. I was trapped in the kitchen. Thoughts of how to "escape" without looking at him quickly came to me. I first thought that I will just sneak out the back door and leave. Then my human arrogance took over and I thought, "I'm not going to fear that man! I may hate him, but I don't fear him!" (That's a contradiction in terms). So I determined that I would walk right out in front of him. I would naturally not say "good bye" or anything. I had never called him "Dad". As I walked in front of him I noticed he had his arms crossed with the TV on and a scowl on his face.

This is where the Holy Spirit took over. He nailed my shoes to the floor just 4 feet from the door knob to the front door, and said firmly, "Darrell, call your Dad "Dad", tell him you love him, and say 'I'll see you later". I told God, "Maybe I can handle the 'I'll see you later' part but never the 'dad' or 'I love you' part". For some reason that I cannot explain or take credit for, I turned to my Dad, walked up to him, reached out my hand to shake his, and said, "Dad, I love you, we'll see you later". Tears came to his eyes, tears came to my eyes and I quickly left. My sister who was still living there said that he never spoke evil of me again...all my Brothers, yes, but not me.

Then I began a seven-year journey of prayer. I began praying for my Dad's Salvation. The devil fought me through all those seemly hopeless prayers telling me that he was selfish and evil and that my prayers for him were a waste of time. Then finally one day, my dad came over and said, "Could I give my life to Christ?" I took the hand that once hit me and we prayed as God ushered him through the veil of Christ's body into salvation. The day I baptized my dad in front of 200 people in a Friend's church in East St. Paul was one of the greatest and most joyous of my life

It doesn't get any better than this!

My mom surrendered her life to Christ in my living room, and my dad began to lead the home in prayer and would take my mom and made a commitment to read the Bible through in a year.

What restored our home was not the work of a Book, a Psychologist, Therapy, or Intervention (as good as those things are). It was the Power of God!

Annie and Martha Paff, Dave and Heidi Chindvall, Mitch Paulson, Lisa Bergeron, Dan Tollefson, Jim Johnson and scads of other wonderful people were a few more key members in the greatest Christian family Minneapolis ever knew. Now some of their kids even support our present ministries in Latin America and India!

There were dozens of stories like this, and I still hear to this day the Testimonies about our radio program, "A Time

Together". People came, they called, they cried, they invited others. It was one of the most exciting times of my life. We would reach out, we would hold Movie Nights for the neighborhood on our front Lawn, and we sometimes would even climb over bodies of those drunk or shot in the Housing Projects as we would cast out demons, and proclaim the Gospel of Christ.

Ellie and I just returned from visiting our life-long friend, Lori Macnamara who we had met when she was just a Teen. She called after a A Time Together Broadcast where the theme was "Faith Alone" on that broadcast. God spoke to her heart and set her free from Legalism. Today her light shines in Las Vegas especially with a Ministry where now volunteers are used to bring church to the elderly in Assisted Care Facilities and Nursing Homes.

Growing up in a dysfunctional home, I was thrilled and intrigued at the Divinely empowered fellowship dynamics of the Body of Christ. We literally become part of one another's life, worship, healing, zeal, revelation, comfort, ministry, and destiny. As we worship, Christ inhabits our presence and moves in the release of giftings for the benefit of one another. What a bold and wonderful life! *"With great power they gave witness of the Lord's resurrection and with glad and sincere hearts they broke bread from house to house and God added to their number daily those who were being saved"*... Acts 3. This life style was a reality to us all and we bear witness to this wonderful era until this day.

We experienced it. And with the old Scottish Revivalists passion we would say, *"If you ever get it, don't let it go!"*

REACHING PEOPLE IS EASY!

Why is it easy? Because people love to be loved! May I encourage you to go about your neighborhood and meet people. Maybe invite them to your home on a certain evening just saying, "hey, c'mon over next Tuesday night to my house. My wife bakes some great cookies and we've got this great informal gathering where anyone can talk and we study parts of the Bible that deal with Life Issues. God's love is really touching some lives. You're invited." People love to be loved! People want your love more than you think. When you're excited about God meeting human needs, people listen!

You're tapping into the greatest love-power under the sun! You too can easily become *"witnesses of the Lord's Resurrection"*...Acts 2

NEW AUTOGRAPH CANDIDATES

We were all just excited about God reaching lives! During these early ministry years, 3 precious new "Autograph Candidates" were born to Ellie & me: Christopher, Timothy, and Michael. I insisted on simple names because I had spelled out my name, letter by letter, to every school teacher since I was five. The memories of these little guys running around carrying on their antics and interacting with the Koinonia family are some of the best memories I have. I remember our camping experiences with them in the summer and playing in the Snow with our Cocker Spaniel in the Winter.

In July of 1982, after 3 years of pastoring, God was stirring my heart. I knew He was going to lead me elsewhere. Although I would rise at 4:30 AM every morning for prayer, I could get no clarity on God's will. At our Bible camp, I spoke to a man I respected, Jim Bradford.

After a brief time of conversation, he assured me that God was calling me to a dedicated season of prayer wherein I would hear the direction of God for my life. I thought to myself, "I wonder if he knows I get up at 4:30 each morning and sort of live a dedicated season of prayer!

Once I shook off the temptations of religious pride, I realized that this was what God Himself was saying to me; so I committed myself to pray and fast the next week. I embraced a great anticipation of hearing God's voice and understanding His direction for me, Ellie, and the kids

The exciting "Brushstrokes" of God keep happening to us and those we love as we keep saying "YES" to God!

Chapter Thirteen

Ashes and Broken Buttons

After 5 years of pastoring, something began to stir in my heart for a new direction. I began a week of seeking the will of God for a whole new direction for my family. I decided to seek the Lord in a more uncomfortable setting: the Basement of my old South Minneapolis House. This basement was a true 1904 basement; no finished areas and it still had the old octopus furnace that had heated the house from when coal was used as fuel. This furnace, though converted to natural gas, still had coal ashes in the bottom of it.

After two days of praying, fasting, and hearing nothing from God I began to get desperate. I remembered in the Old Testament how holy men would "rend their clothes" and put on "sack cloth and ashes" as they would bare their souls to God. In my desperation I went to the furnace, opened up the big cast iron door and took a handful of ashes and spread them on my face and clothes. Then I cried out to God, "I have to know what you want, God! I have to hear you!" Still no answer. Surely as the days go by I will hear God's voice or get some kind of Divine Guidance. I thought, well, the ashes didn't work, I'll try 'rending my clothes'", but I knew my wife would kill me if I ruined a good shirt, so I looked for something that resembled "Sackcloth"-I guess I still don't know what it is! I went to my work clothes area and put on an old flannel shirt. I grabbed it and tore the two halves apart and the buttons went flying. I went through other 'sackcloth shirts during the week. I repeated, "God, I have to hear you". My wife would hear me and yell down the stairs, "Darrell, are you ok?" I thought to myself how hilarious the scene would look to someone. Here is a guy in a Basement with black ash all over him wearing torn clothes with no buttons and talking very loudly to God. I'm glad my wife didn't have me committed!

But you know what? God began to speak to me. Now I'm not recommending this as some formula for hearing from God, but God said, *"You'll search for me and find me when you search for me with all you heart"* and in Proverbs 2 he said, *"When you lift up your voice and cry out for understanding, you'll get it."* God always wants first place and He shows himself strong to those *"whose hearts are totally given to Him"*

> **"You'll search for me and find me when you search for me with all your heart"**
> **Jeremiah 29:13**

During special and creative relational times with God, He may speak directly like he did to me. Other times He may not speak as directly, but you see that He is guiding your thoughts, your pen, or your understanding of the Word. It's almost like a "flow" of Personal Revelation inside of your mind and heart. I don't know how else to describe it.

Once in a rare while, He speaks through Angels, trances, dreams, or personal appearances. Still other times, it may seem like he doesn't speak at all! I've had those times, but then you notice the 'pay back' after you end the fast. You feel a confidence in your decisions and you know that *"the steps of a good man (you) are being ordered by the Lord"*

My seeking heart was about to discover something that I didn't expect! It was to be the next critical Autographing of my heart. He couldn't reveal to me what I wanted to know and He couldn't release me into a greater place of ministry until this Autographing was done.

Well, here's what the Lord said: "Call all of the people you've offended in your life and ask them for forgiveness" I said, "Say what! God, I want to know where I'm supposed to go and what I'm supposed to do with my life! What's this about calling people I've offended?" God began showing me people and situations out of the past. He wanted me to make a list. The list was long!!! I knew that I was supposed to go to the phone and call these people. I still argued with God: "God, some of these people really hurt me!!! I was only defending myself! I was only like 10% to blame!" Well, we know that God doesn't play the numbers game. He said, "Darrell, you had no control over what they did, but you had total control over what you did. Call them and ask them to find it in their heart to forgive you!"

The responses were mixed as you can imagine. Some were so happy that they would cry and say, "of course I forgive you. Would you forgive me? Thank you so much for calling, I love you etc, etc".

Others were not so sure and acted like it was about time I called, but they did forgive me. It was a little like walking on eggs sometimes, and I was careful not to begin new arguments. Only one person would not forgive me. To this day, I carry this burden.

God's love & wisdom in this way is wonderful. Why does He make us "clean up" relationships? First of all, He is determined to teach us how important relationships are to Him. Secondly, He wants us to build a new Ministry on a healthy foundation. He doesn't want all the hurt people of the past sort of just floating out there! Besides that, be aware that the Bible says that *"your Sins will find you out"*. You don't want to be waiting for some bad story to surface.

Since many people (especially non-believers) won't receive truth and they are very offense oriented, your attempts at trying to get your point of view understood are usually futile. That's why you just have to apologize for what you did wrong...period! Don't try to "set the record straight". It will just start another cat fight. When Jesus hung on the cross after being unduly and unjustly tortured and humiliated, He just said, "Father, forgive them for they know not what they do". He recognized that there is a time to forgive rather than state his case. He recognized that people are so deceived when they live by their feelings that really believe that what they're doing is right; that they very literally *"know not what they do"* like Jesus said when He forgave all those who were jeering at Him while He hung on the cross! Jesus restored Relationships at His cost! He does it still today, because His Sacrifice was for all sins of all time! He recognized that forgivingness is always more important than "being understood".

ONE OF THE GREAT OPPORTUNITIES

Do we realize what an opportunity Forgiveness and Restoration are? Matthew 18 says it literally opens the power of heaven when we do what Christ did. Relational agreement literally binds evil things from happening and loosens good things to happen in our lives. Millions around the world are living devoid of the blessing and grace of Heaven because of their foolish Pride. Unforgiveness is like the unpaid bills of personal vindictiveness. But we never get even with those who hurt us by unforgiveness. It only hurts us! It's like locking ourselves in a prison and saying, "I'll get even with you". People that do that live their whole life in misery trying to get even or insist they are right and then after many years of misery they go to a meaningless Grave.

You have the opportunity and power to restore a relationship today! Get up and by the love of God, do it now!

During that week of seeking God in the basement I learned two vital things for life:
1. I learned the great truth of Hebrew 11:6, *"God is a rewarder of those who <u>diligently</u> seek Him"*. A Little seeking/A little reward; lots of seeking/ lots of rewards! God is not like a 14 year old infatuated school girl. He never waves His arms in your direction and shouts, "here I am!" His love is like His mystery...its wonderful! He must be sought out with great energy and then He will be wondrously discovered. He's worth the search!
2. I also learned that God doesn't release you into anointed Ministry until you've cleaned up your relational messes! He's serious about this! Read Matthew 18. You've got to learn and appreciate and apply relational principles. In the list of 7 things the Lord hates in Proverbs, only one is a person! *"He who sows discord among the Brethren"*. This is not some optional thing. Is breathing optional? Neither is it a time based thing. We embrace it now and we get on with it now. We abandon Gossip, Offence,

Unforgivness, and Pride today and as we do it, God almighty will grant your life new power. He did in mine!

On the 4th day, once I got all the relational stuff cleaned up from my past, I went back down in the basement and God started speaking to me about the nation of Guatemala. I didn't even know where it was! I got out a map. "Oh, here it is right underneath Mexico", I muttered to myself.

Our family was to be Missionaries to Guatemala

Chapter Fourteen

Operation Love Lift

I arrived at church, got off my Motorcycle and walked inside for a great service; then I saw the table at the back of the Foyer. Oh no! Elephant Tusks! I considered sneaking back out! I did not want to hear another boring Missionary in frumpy clothes drone on about eating monkey meat! Similar events had happened a number of times in my early Christian years. I just felt like Missionaries were sort of irrelevant to my Christian frame of reference!

My call to Guatemala was now bringing me into that strange and "irrelevant" club of..."Missionary"!!!

A Songwriter, Keith Green died in July of 82. His life had had a great impact on me. The summer before he died, he did a tour of Missionary bases in other countries. At the time the whole thing seemed a bit strange. He had planned an American concert tour that was to incorporate this vision, and then his death happened before he began it. A group called Youth With A Mission teamed up with his ministry and his widow, Melody, and did the tour anyway with a video tape of Keith at "Jesus West Coast" They called it the Keith Green Memorial tour.

Well, I was attending with Ellie and some people from the church that I pastored. I was looking for ways that the Lord might speak to me about my call to Guatemala. The presentation deeply moved me about the need of World Missions. After the concert and presentation, they invited those who were interested in serving to get in lines giving out info on different parts of the World. I knew that Guatemala was in Central America so I got in that line. I waited and waited while looking back over toward the people of my church as they were wondering what their pastor was doing in this line to get info on going to Central America!!! Someone finally came along and handed me information on some training school in New Hampshire and I thought "this is silly, I've got to be a responsible pastor and go back with my people and get going home".

GOD CLARIFIES THE CALL & MIRACULOUSLY PROVIDES

Then the Lord spoke clearly to my heart to go up to a certain individual who I didn't know at all. I said to myself "why Lord?" He said, "Do it now". So I went up and began talking to this man whose name was Glenn Price. He turned out to be on staff with Youth With A Mission (the organization that sponsored the event in partnership with Keith Green's ministry). I shared with him that I was a Pastor, blah blah and small talk. I kept sheepishly glancing over at my church people. All the time I was speaking to Glenn, the Spirit of God was saying, "ask him about Guatemala, ask him about Guatemala!"

I thought to myself "that would be silly, what would he know about this strange call I had to a place I never knew and to do something I've never done! Finally the pressure from God was too great and I blurted out, "do you know anything about Guatemala?" He replied, "Do I ever! I'm the Director of an International event called Operation

Love Lift which will bring hundreds of people from all over the world to Guatemala in January!!!

I got information and went home feeling excited about being part of this "Love Lift" event! I finally informed my church about what I was feeling. They agreed to take up an offering at a future service. What I didn't tell them was that I needed an initial down payment within a few days. I needed $600. I felt like God would provide this, so, **I told no one**. I needed this money by Dec 1st. It was Nov 30 and I called ahead and told the Missions team leader that I had not received the down payment and would therefore have to cancel my plans to be part of his Missions Team to Guatemala. A few hours later, I saw someone walking around on our front lawn. I called my wife over to the living room window and said, "Who is that?" She said, "It looks like Frank Matejak" (a church member). He continued to orbit our lawn and appeared in deep thought. Finally we saw him come toward the front door. He knocked; we answered, and said, "Oh, hi Frank, how ya doin?" He responded, "I can't explain it you guys, but I feel led to give you this". It was $600. **It was a miraculous provision. He knew nothing about our need.**

Well the church took up an offering a few weeks later. The Church Secretary notified me that the offering was $450. short of what I needed. We had already had a going-away party and it was New Year's Eve day. I told my wife, "I have to leave tomorrow and I cant' go because I'm $450 short. I can't leave without this money"!

To make matters worse, Minneapolis had just had the biggest Snow Storm in years and everything was buried with 20 inches of snow. This just added to my sense of "God, where are you?" I was ready to call the Mission again and tell them I wouldn't be there. I thought "this is embarrassing! Where are you God?"

Then I got a surprise phone call. I said, "Hello?" The young male voice on the end asked the question, "Hi, do you still have the 1962 Buick for sale?" I said, "How do you know that I have a 1962 Buick?" (I had a 1962 Buick and it had been posted for sale in July of that year, but I didn't have one response from the Newspaper Ad. It had been over 5 months since I gave up on selling it and it had been parked in a Snow bank at my Dad and Mom's place in a suburb of Minneapolis.)

He said, "Well I saw the ad last summer and I didn't call and suddenly today I'm very interested in the car, and would like to look at it if you still have it" I almost dropped the phone as I was looking out the living room window at the cars buried up to their windows in snow. I said, You're kidding me right? He said, "No". I told him where it was in my Mom's driveway in St. Louis Park, MN. And I told him that he should go over, get the key from my Mom, unbury it from the snow and give me a call if he's still interested in it.

After I hung up I thought, "oh no, maybe this was God's way of providing for my mission trip and I sort of blew it and let him go. One hour later the man calls. He says, "I'm here at your mom's, I started it up, and it's exactly what I want". I felt led to not tell him a price. Instead I said, "How much will you give me for it?" His response nearly floored me. He said, "Would you take 450 dollars? Tears ran down my cheeks. I consoled myself and said, "Yes, I will". He said I'll be right over with the money. He arrived an hour later and counted out 450 dollars cash into my hand...exactly what I needed. I said to my family...well, I guess I'm going to Guatemala!"

The greatest experiences I've had and most miraculous Divine provision I've seen have come as I've made myself available to World Missions.

IT ACTUALLY HAPPENS

My time serving with the Arkansas YWAM Missions Team in Guatemala was the most wonderful experience of my life. I saw more miracles in those two months than I had seen in my whole life. I led many to Christ. I'd never seen such an open-to-Christ culture. I could go out any time and lead people to Christ. We had to hide our Gospel tracts as we traveled on the bus or sat in a restaurant. People would come up and ask for them!

> *"The greatest experiences I've had and most miraculous Divine provision I've seen have come as I've made myself available to World Missions."*

The trip culminated with me being asked to be part of a Mercy Ministry Team to a remote Indian Area called the Ixil Triangle up in the beautiful highlands of Guatemala. It had recently been cleared of Insurgents although there was still much military activity there. We were driving a large Diesel-powered Flatbed Truck loaded with construction supplies. We sent the truck on its way the day before and we were set to rendezvous with it by Bus the following day. We were given papers by the president himself that we were to present at any roadblocks, or military checkpoints. We were informed that traveling at night was not an option and to look out for Insurgent Guerillas. A Wycliffe missionary that had been forced to leave the area briefed us on these facts. I asked him, "How do we know an insurgent when we see them?" He replied, "It is difficult because sometimes they kill the soldiers and take their clothes and pose as Guatemalan soldiers. The Team's eyes met in an obvious look of concern. Then he replied with a comment he decided was helpful, "we heard that the guerillas just received a shipment of Vinyl Military boots from Europe. If they have vinyl boots, they for sure are Insurgents. It was almost hilarious during the checkpoints. All of our eyes went for the boots!!!

We arrived in the province of Quiche after a 4-hour Bus ride. We were herded out of the bus by a dozen solders and separated from the other passengers and ordered to stand against a wall in an alley. I thought to myself, "They're going to shoot us!" We waited for about 30 minutes while some of the soldiers took our papers and disappeared into a walled compound. A few of the soldiers stayed to guard us. The 30 minutes seemed like forever. Finally a guard arrived and escorted us into the compound. I thought "they're going to shoot us in there where no one will hear!!!" We were ushered into what I'm sure was the swankiest room on the base. Red carpeting and a big Mahogany Desk and an officer with a burgundy beret greeted us warmly, "well, you're pretty important people". I innocently responded, "We are?" He said, "Yes, I had to verify these papers. When I saw them, I knew you were either very important or this was the biggest hoax I've ever seen. I'm adding a special note and my own seal at the bottom to make sure you don't have any problems going up to the Ixil Triangle"

Whoa, this was great! The truck had also been cleared and was waiting outside so we jumped on board and began 2 days of driving that I'll never forget. We drove this huge heavy fully loaded truck over trees pushed down to form bridges over ravines and raging rivers, we were breaking down often---mostly vapor lock, but it created long delays and we were remembering the Missionaries words, "driving at night is not an option". We would meet other vehicles on these narrow dirt roads carved from the side of a high mountain. I would try to console myself by saying, "well, many vehicles do this and none of them roll off the road and down the Mountain". Then I looked down the Mountain and it did anything but reassure me...there was a Bus way down there smashed and on its side. "Whoa, they do roll off!" From that point I would always be on the inside edge of the truck fully prepared to jump to safety if it began to fall off the Road.

Well it got dark and I remember looking up at the Stars and Constellations and thinking, "They are the same ones I see from my back yard at home". I wondered if Ellie was looking at those same stars back home and suddenly I felt a strange security in the connection in believing she was. Suddenly we saw the lights of a small town in the distant valley. One of the Guatemalans said, "Nebaj". That was to be the name of the town that was our destination that night. In the town there was one Motel...or should we say "place of lodging". It was called "Las Tres Hermanas". The Three Sisters. It was a place of hospitality run by three Catholic Nuns. They warmly greeted us and we were so glad to have made it to this haven without being met by any Guerillas. My weary body was ready for a good nights sleep. I lay down on the bed that was warmly provided by the nuns and it felt like the Atlantic Ocean frozen over. I lifted the two inch thick mattress and noticed it was set on 1 x 4 wood planks set about a foot apart. After trying this for a while, I just put the mattress on the floor and took my chances with whatever living creatures may roam there once the lights were out. The hot water for showers was this unique arrangement of coiled pipe running through an open fire outside and one of the "sisters" was outside stoking this fire bright and early. I opened the valve on the shower and was greeted by a huge gush of high-powered steam followed by the hottest water this side of Yellowstone Park. I went in for breakfast, and one of these wonderful hostesses said, "How do you want your eggs cooked". I looked around at the unsanitary conditions of this kitchen and replied, "boiled"!

It was a beautiful day and we got an early start and headed for the second point of our triangle called Chajul. This is where I was to be stationed doing electrical wiring preparation for a medical clinic that was being established there to help the Indigenous peoples of that area. As we drove in, I had to do a double-take at the native people's culture. On my right was a "road crew" with picks and shovels. They were the Chajul men who had all white clothes with a red sash around their middle. They took off there broad hats and wiped the perspiration off of there heads as they greeted us with a wave. On my other side was a beautiful River with women washing corn and clothes. They had brightly colored native garb. We entered the village and found the place that had been acquired for us to turn into a "Medical Facility".

The scenes of a war zone in rural Guatemala were a story to remember. The Military was in firm control of our area, but you could hear the battles in the distance every night. One day some "Guerillas" had surrendered. They didn't look like Guerillas. They were families-with kids,- even with babies! They had been told that the military would kill them if they surrendered so they had fought on until they were skin and bones, so decimated by starvation and disease that they just gave up. They were not treated with death, but instead with food, medical care, and respect. Doctors brought in from Guatemala City could not believe that there were American civilians up there.

I know there is much controversy surrounding the Presidency of Efrain Rios Montt in those years, but I witnessed things more closely than most and I saw his leadership bring stability, morality, unity, and victory to a nation that was on the brink of collapse.

My work was joyous and I was never so fulfilled in my life using my practical giftings to prep this place so that Doctors and Dentists could be flown in to help these people, who for centuries were decimated by illness and never had any help. You should have seen the "Air Strip" that had been carved out of the mountain forest by the Indians. It was to be a 30-minute plane ride from Guatemala City once this thing was completed. The only other access was a 2 day truck drive like we knew. I thought to myself, "I'd choose the truck drive rather than land on this thing, even with the driving across tree trunks and skinny hairpin mountain curves".

The Lord God painted new and wonderful strokes on the canvas of my life.

Chapter Fifteen

Wayne Snyder

February 21, 1983 was the most profound day of Destiny and Divine Guidance of my life. Our work was done in the Ixil Triangle; we boarded the now empty Truck for the trip back. We wanted to do all the travel in one day, so we left at 6 AM to try to make it to Quiche by 3PM to catch a bus to Guatemala City and arrive by nightfall. We hoped that the vapor lock problem would be done since we were now empty of heavy materials and going downhill.

We began our trip home through the beautiful lush highlands of Guatemala and watched the morning mist rise over the mountain tops. Even though the truck was very noisy, the serene beauty almost made it seem quiet. I was standing up in the bed of the vehicle holding on to this pipe that served as a hand rail around the perimeter of the rear of the truck. It was there I heard of the voice of the Lord. "You will resign from your church; give them a two-month notice". I responded to God, "how can I do that, it's my only money! I need that money to live!" God responded, "Did I call you to feed off of the sheep or to feed the sheep?" I didn't even bother telling God that I sort of planned to do both! I knew that if I stayed at the Church that I would be half-hearted in that work and therefore wouldn't feed the Sheep like I should. They needed a different shepherd! I said, "What then, God?" All the Lord said was "You need to contact Wayne Snyder"

Now, Wayne Snyder was a person who I had met only once, 5 years before, in Bozeman, Montana at a church that he pastored. When God told me the name, He must have helped me remember the person! My wife and I and our 6 month old first-born, Chris, had taken a one-month celebration tour of the western states in our 1957 Chrysler, after I had graduated from College. We were in a Motel in Bozeman and it was Sunday. I said, let's go to Church". We looked up an Assembly of God Church in Bozeman and attended the service, and after that were greeted by the pastor (who wasn't even the Preacher that morning). I shook his hand and asked him if he knew of a Doctor because Chris had the sniffles and he was our first born and a parent always gets very concerned about any sign of sickness with his firstborn. He pointed out a doctor who was just coming out of the sanctuary! The Doctor assured us that everything would be ok with Chris –just keep him warm, and we were on our way...that's it!

That's all I ever knew of Wayne Snyder! I can't even remember him telling me his name. I have no clue how I knew who he was when God told me to contact him.

So, back to Guatemala. We arrived to Quiche just as the bus was leaving. I literally ran to catch it. I was feeling very culturally confident at the time and opened up the back door of the bus by myself to throw my stuff in there. As I placed my heavy backpack on the top of the heap of other stuff, I heard the muffled attempts of some chickens in a bag to free themselves from this new weight that had been thrown on top of them. I moved my stuff over a bit to relieve them, although I'm sure their demise was imminent anyway! I smiled to myself as I remembered how the term "Chicken Bus" had come into existence among us Gringos.

We share buses with birds and animals! I also had not had time to take a potty break in the hubbub to catch the Bus so by now I really had to go! I thought, well, the driver will stop somewhere. Instead, he just kept picking up people until there were 7 people across each set of two seats that had been meant for 4. The center guy just straddled the two seats with a "cheek" on the edge of both seats. It was a great experience. How can you not love Guatemala? Well, my love for the culture didn't make my bladder any emptier. I looked at my watch and thought, "Hallelujah, its only one more hour to Guatemala City". Then I heard the men in the seat in front of me talking and one of them said, "Tres horas a Guatemala". That's "3 hours to Guatemala". I almost died. When the bus finally reached Guatemala City, I flew off the bus and ran to the nearest Hotel and…

I was feeling so empowered, victorious, & confident after this life changing time concluded with God's direction. In 4 days, I would go home to share my stories, see my wife, see my kids, and to call Wayne Snyder!

That night I got something bad. I felt like I was going to die. I would drag myself out of my sleeping bag only to go to the toilet. I was sweating and literally thought, "This is what it feels like to die". I prayed it would go away. People came in and prayed some wonderful loving prayers. Most of them began with "Lord, if it be thy will to heal Darrell…" I remained the same. I imagined being hospitalized and canceling my plane flight home. Then this young English brother came in with fire in his eyes. He was sent by God. He fastened his eyes on me and with great confidence just stooped down to where I was on the floor in my bag and placed his hand on my head and with great volume said, "Lord, we vindicate your name oh great God". Then he looked at me and said, "Be healed in the name of Jesus". Then he stood up and said, "How do you feel?" I said, "I don't know" as I assessed my body's feelings after being so sick and then being shaken by this young man's visit. I said, "I think I'm better." Then I got up and walked around. "I'm a lot better! Wow, I'm healed, Hallelujah!" I immediately packed my things and the next day flew home with great victory in my heart!

My reunion with Ellie and the kid's was divine. Ellie had a beautiful place all set up complete with violin and candles and romance at this great Italian restaurant, but I couldn't shut up about Guatemala! I even brought back some of the "artifacts" and was telling Ellie about the culture and the miracles. She finally said, "Darrell, you've been gone for two months to Guatemala, can't we talk about something else?" I learned a lesson that evening that I've taught to hundreds of others when they are done with Missions trips. Don't expect those who weren't there to share your enthusiasm! And that's ok! Just be patient and share it in shorter Sound Bites over several weeks.

You better believe that the next day I was digging up the phone number for a certain church in Montana! My phone call went like this:

> Church: Hello, Bozeman Assembly of God"
> Me: Hi my name is Darrell Dobbelmann, I'd like to talk to Pastor Snyder.
> Church: Pastor Snyder is no longer with us"
> Me: Do you have a phone number for him?"
> Church: (Background noise.) Secretary asking others "does anyone know where Pastor Snyder lives now? Blah, blah, Hello,... Mr. Dobbelmann? We have no contact information of Pastor Snyder. Someone here believes he moved out southwest somewhere to pastor another church"
> Me: "Thank you, good, by"

My heart sank. I then thought, I'll look in my book of Assembly of God ministers! I looked and his name did not appear! What should I do? My whole life sort of hung on this "Word" that I thought was from the Lord. "Get a-hold of Wayne Snyder" How? This was before the days of the internet and Yahoo People Searches.

Ellie and I visited her folks with the kids to sort of have a reunion after what I think they perceived as sort of a "Crazy Trip". We had a nice meal and then Ellie's Dad asked me to step out on the front porch, and with his quiet English dignity exhorted me to question the things I was pursuing. To him, me quitting my job, then pastoring, and now talking about Missions in Guatemala was taking things in the wrong direction. We had struggled for money from the time I had quit my job to go into Ministry full-time. He finished his talk with me by leaning forward in his chair toward me and with his quiet but determined English dignity said, "Darrell, why don't you get a real job like normal men and support my daughter?"

Those words were to be used by the devil many times over the next few months. They were like a knife in my side. Wounds I could not get rid of. He was well-meaning of course. I went to God and said, "Lord, I thought this was your voice I was hearing? You say Wayne Snyder, and where is he? Then the knife twisted and I remembered the words, and I linked them with words from the Bible like *"He who doesn't provide for his own is worse than an Infidel"* Am I worse than an Infidel Lord?

I put my two-month notice in at my Church and was headed to absolutely nothing. I had no savings; I had only one of my beloved Classic Cars left over from my "rich days". Once I sell that, then we would be penniless. I was hanging my hat on what I thought I was sure was God's voice. My Dad-in-laws' words were remembered and the knife was felt again.

After a few months, I was done with my church, and in the biggest No-Man's Land of my life...ever been there? One night, I felt led to rise early in the middle of the night and go down to Lake of the Isles to pray. God had spoken to me many times in this place. He spoke again. "Darrell, go to Lindale Texas". I said, "Now I know this isn't you Lord... go to Lindale? Lindale, Texas is a Christian Mecca! I'm just job hunting! This is my subconscious mind speaking to me."

He didn't even answer, but then said, "Oh, Darrell, before you go, keep that promise to your wife & kids". I thought, what promise? Oh yeah, I had promised them I would take them camping. I put my last classic car up for sale- a 1954 Chrysler Station Wagon. There were only 1100 of them made and I had poured my time into the restoration of it...Oh well. I remember seeing it being driven down the alley and me having the last $1500. of my life in my hand.

I borrowed my Sisters' new little gas efficient Plymouth and loaded up my family for the North Shore of Lake Superior for a camping get-away. We had a great time. Although a bear almost ate our Cocker Spaniel, but that story is for another time.

My trip to Texas had a sense of destiny to it. I realized that I must be looking pretty foolish to people...following these Voices I "hear", but I didn't care right now. I arrived at the YWAM base where I had set up lodging and a tour. The lady said, ""you'll have the Dorm all to yourself. The whole school just left for ministry in Guatemala". Hmmmm.

HITTING BOTTOM

I woke the next morning and felt hopeful. I went on the YWAM tour of the Base and its' Programs. The facilities were beautiful, but I <u>wasn't</u> surprised that I <u>wasn't</u> feeling called there. If I was to go to YWAM, I would have gone with those at the Arkansas base that I developed relationship with in Guatemala. In fact, if I was to follow my feelings, I felt flat out called to the Arkansas base and its work in Guatemala. What was I doing here? But God told me to go to Texas, not Arkansas. Also, whenever I would bring "Youth With A Mission" up with others they would furrow their brow and get a real concerned tone in their voice and say something like, "Darrell you're not a youth, why would you go to Youth With A Mission", or would say, "Darrell, didn't you already get training at a Bible College? Why would you go to a Training School? Didn't you already spend 4 years preparing for Ministry?", or, "Won't this be very hard on your Family?", or "Darrell, don't you need money now!!!" And the remembering of my Father-in-law's words would follow close on the heels of theirs.

I jumped in my car and visited all the other Ministries hoping I could "find a job". I talked to lots of leaders and people. I even tried to visit Dave Wilkerson's World Challenge, but there was a sign in the driveway that said, "NO TRESSPASSING" Oh well, I guess God doesn't want me there.

I toured Last Days Ministries last, because it was the Ministry that sponsored the Memorial Concert that spoke to my heart so strongly, and I thought for sure that this was the place God would give me an "in" for my new Life and Ministry. That proved to be a naïve thought. Our tour group was led around the facilities. My heart was pounding inside. When he was showing us the Printing Operation, I wanted to blurt out, "I don't want to see Printing presses. My Father-in-law is telling me to get a real job; I'm hearing voices that I think are from God, my family is out of money, and I'm like... ready to die!" As the tour ended, and the Tour Guides' hand was on the door knob, I again wanted to scream, "don't open the door, I need a job here!"

I walked out that lonely door with my proverbial tail between my legs---I remember seeing the color of the sidewalk; it looked new. I saw this Plane with its wings tied down, I got into my Sister's car and wondered; and wondered. I drove over to the Dairy Queen that I had seen earlier. I bought myself one of those things you eat when you get depressed and feel like the World is ending. What's it called? Oh yes, a "Hot fudge Brownie Delight". The problem is, you can't eat it forever! Though I lingered, I now scraped the last of the Hot Fudge off of the inside bottom of the container.

I literally felt like a whipped Puppy. I couldn't feel any more like a Looser. I returned to the YWAM Dorm room and thought, "at least I'll have that whole dorm room all to myself, I don't want to se or talk to anyone right now". It was only 4PM, but I pondered the Wayne Snyder thing, the Lindale Texas thing, and the words of my Father-in-law. I literally could not wait for the Sun to set. I would go to bed, rise early, make my trip back home, and use the remainder of the $1500. to live on until I could go request my job back at my old Plastics firm. I hoped they would take me. Well, I'll get some kind of job and start to make some money. Enough of this hearing-the-voice-of-God business. I must be mad!

THE STRANGER!

I settled into the lonely Dorm Room. It fit my mood perfectly. Right then, a very talkative man came into the room. He was exactly the kind of man you don't want to meet when you are severely depressed! He notified me that he was spending the night, and I thought Oh No!

He talked on and on about visiting the ministries in the area. I could have cared less! He talked about how he had dug up the locations of all these Christian Musicians and visited them. He had even snooped around and found Melody Green's (Keith Green's widow) House and tried to visit her but said he was disappointed to find she was not at home. He talked so much that we had not even shared each others' names or introduced ourselves to one another. Finally he looked me squarely in the eye and said "Hey, you're Darrell Dobbelmann aren't you!" Surprisingly I said, "Yes! How did you know that?" He said, "I was a DJ at KUXL in Mpls., and I would play your recorded Radio Shows 'A Time Together', Wow; they were a real blessing to me!" Then he kept on talking, "I've been down here Job hunting". I responded, "Boy, I guess I have too". He said, I'm in radio and I searched all over Dallas and Fort Worth and found nothing, so I came here sort of depressed". Again I agreed, "Yeah, I know that feeling".

Then he said something that changed my life! He said, "I visited World Challenge." I uttered, "How did you do that, it says no trespassing on the gate?" He stated confidently, "Oh you don't let signs like that stop you." He continued his story, "I wanted to meet Dave Wilkerson so I drove up and went inside. There was a man at the Desk whose name was _____.

165

Guess what the name was of the guy at the desk? <u>It was Wayne Snyder</u>!

I tried to console myself as I looked up World Challenges' number in the local Phone Directory. I kept saying to myself, "I'm not going to get my hopes up. There's more than one Wayne Snyder in the World!" I fumbled the receiver; my hands were sweaty; my heart was pounding as a voice came over the line, "Good afternoon, this is World Challenge". I tried to control myself, but blurted out impatiently, "I need to talk to Wayne Snyder!" He gently responded, "I'm Wayne Snyder, can I help you?" I quickly asked, "Are you the Wayne Snyder who pastored in Bozeman, Montana five years ago?" He said, "Why, yes I am; who's this?" I told him, "I need to talk to you right now. I'll come right down". He said, "We were just closing". I begged him, "You must stay there, please, and I'll be right down". He agreed.

I got in my car and drove down the road and past the infamous "No Trespassing" sign. Wayne showed me to a room and I poured out my heart to him about Guatemala, no money, God's voice, Father-in-laws, and my desire to join YWAM Arkansas except for all the warnings & bewilderments of family and friends.

Wayne, it turned out had had a Ministry career similar to mine. He said, *"Darrell, I too went to Bible College, pastored for 3 years like you, had three small kids, and then felt led to go to Youth With A Mission in my mid 30's. Everybody discouraged me, but God was leading me so I ignored all the negative advice and went; and it was fantastic! I'd strongly encourage you to go to YWAM Arkansas".*

I asked how he had disappeared off the Radar Screen of life, and I told him it was a miracle that God had now led me to him here. How on earth did he get from Bozeman, Montana to Lindale, Texas working for Dave Wilkerson? He said after he had left the church in Bozeman, Montana that he went to New Mexico and took a church that after a while decided to leave the Assemblies of God. The District leadership had a policy that if a church does that; the pastor must give up his ministerial credentials. That's why his name was not in my book of Assemblies of God Ministers. He said that he had developed Brain Cancer in New Mexico and after much debilitating medical treatment; he was given the prognosis of "Terminal". He quit his church to be with his wife the last months of his life. Dave Wilkerson had heard about Wayne's dilemma, and invited him to move to the beautiful setting of East Texas to finish out his days in a non-demanding ministry position of answering letters written to World Challenge. Wayne informed me that the drugs he was being treated with made him "look like a chipmunk" and made him very sick and so he just quit them. Rather than getting worse, miraculously, his cancer went into remission. He said he was supposed to have died years ago! All the doctors were amazed.

It was not yet 6PM. Fewer than 2 hours ago, I was broken, whipped, discouraged, and finished with ministry. I was done hearing the voice of God, and I was going to give up and get my old job back. Now...in a moment, everything was turned around!

I once heard a sermon called *"The Miracle of the Zero Factor"*. The gist of it was that God makes stuff out of nothing" *"We understand that the things which are seen were not made of things which do appear"*. And there is another scripture: Hebrews 11:1 *"Faith is the substance of things hoped for and the evidence of things which are not seen yet"*. Always remember that we have a God who "does stuff" in us! Phil 2:13-*"It is God who worketh in us both to do and to will...".* When it seems as though we are at the end of our rope, that's when God begins to do <u>His</u> thing.

The next morning dawned; there was a song on my lips. I left quietly so I wouldn't stir my friend who had been such an agent of God for my life. What if he wouldn't have said, "...whose name was Wayne Snyder". I whispered a, "God Bless you", and prayed as I walked toward the door that God would bless him with a miracle too. To this day I wonder if this stranger was an angel!

The morning could not have been any more beautiful! The birds seemed even clearer in their songs. The smells of flowers couldn't have been any sweeter. God had pulled all of it together in one moment. I now had clear leading.

I was to go to YWAM training in Arkansas and after that I was to go to Guatemala!

Now listen to this. A few weeks after my visit with Wayne, his cancer came back with a vengeance and he was dead in a matter of weeks. The sense of timing and destiny was profound!

Jesus was using His "Pen" in my life again!

Chapter Sixteen

The "Ambassadors"

Leaving the house that had represented stability to me for over 30 years was like an Abraham and Sarah moment. "Take your wife and children and some of your things and leave the home of your youth" seemed to be the call!

2303 Girard Ave. S. was where I grew up while my biological dad was alive and after my mom remarried and moved out, she retained it as rental property. It was still owned by my mom and after my step-dad had kicked me out of his house, I moved into the garage. Then as soon as one of the 1st floor opened up (it was a duplex) I moved back in. When I got married, I moved my wife in and we had our first three kids there. Being the house I grew up in, it had many memories of the stable years that my dad was alive. I remember playing with our cocker pups out in the yard while my mom would sing and hang laundry outside. I remember the sound of old propeller driven airplanes flying overhead. It was indeed an idyllic story of life in the fifties. It was the only place on earth that represented the stability and fun from the era before my Dad died.

Now my wife and I and our children were to leave and be Ambassadors to another Nation

My Father-in-law was purposeful in telling me he disagreed with my decision to be a missionary, but I loved him and understood his concerns. The command to *"Honor your Father and Mother"* can be fulfilled in other ways that explicit obedience when one comes of age! He was a stately Englishman who always tried to avoid hardship. He brought me out on his porch and said, "Darrell, when you left your good job to be a Pastor; that was one step in the wrong direction. Your decision to be a Missionary is another step in the wrong direction!" I mentioned the rest of what he said in a previous chapter. But, I had heard from God! We had to obey and leave!

I had gotten my papers to report for duty and I had no other choice.

His words did not fall on un-hearing ears! I was finally living in the home that I grew up in and that represented security to me. I had recovered from the insecurity of the past, and had a wonderful new identity in my life. Ellie and the kids had helped me to discover what life is. I was about to walk away from everything that represented security and in spite of the furrowed brows of my loved ones, walk into nations at war and bring my family into the middle of it. God was to deepen the significance of His Autograph upon our lives and many others. You see, when you choose His ways, your life inevitably impacts other lives and begins becoming a part of many other "Autographs".

I sold my old classic cars and other belongings. My neighbor bought my 1954 Buick Skylark convertible. I already told you about the 1954 Chrysler Wagon. I gave my mom the 1957 Chrysler. Years later she gave it back. I still have it! This was the car I drove to both Coasts as a hippie to do anti-war protests. It's the car I traveled in around the country to do George McGovern's Presidential campaigning. It then transitioned my time of salvation and the time of reordering of my values and was the car I courted Ellen in and then even took it on our honeymoon. It serves as a wonderful memory to my marriage, and to the privilege of my early family years. My kids are all grown now and I have many Grandkids...but the Chrysler is still the same.

In October of 1983, we loaded up our last car, a 1967 Buick LeSabre and hooked my dad's trailer to it and took off for Elm Springs, Arkansas for three months of training with Youth With A Mission before leaving for Guatemala.

We had my precious 3 sons: Chris who was 5, Tim who was 3, and Mike who was barely 2. During one of our prayer times God spoke to Ellie and said, "You're ready for a girl". A few weeks later, Ellie was pregnant with what was to be our only and beloved girl, Amanda.

The training time was a huge change from our previous Pastoral lifestyle, but very enjoyable. It was just like Wayne Snyder told me it would be. The truths and experiences we learned during the YWAM Discipleship Training School (DTS) changed our lives and prepared us for our futures.

Training ended just before Christmas and Ellie discovered she was pregnant about the same time. This turned out to be the girl that God said Ellie was ready for. The leaders gave us a week off for Christmas before we were to take off to Guatemala. We decided to drive the 600 miles home to Minnesota before we left for Guatemala. We took a Swedish gal and a gal from Green Bay with us. Christmas was great with our families and we rejoiced together even though they were concerned about us going to war-torn Guatemala with the small boys and a pregnant wife.

We left Minnesota on January 2nd at 4AM. We were to leave on the 4th for Guatemala, so we were pressed for time. At 6AM, I gave the driving to Ellie and closed my eyes for a well-deserved nap. Not 10 minutes later, I was awakened with a dreadful knocking sound in the motor. As a mechanic, I know a connecting rod was going out and we would not make it more than a few miles. I pulled into a gas station and put in 3 cans of STP so we could limp it to a place to get a used car. We didn't have much money and all cars sold in Iowa were upgraded to meet State standards and were very expensive. I asked a man at a car lot if there was another way out. The man responded, "Well, if you get a red tag car, but then you have to upgrade it within a month before you can license it". He told me there was a "red tag" guy over in Mason City. We arrived and the owner said, "Well, I ain't got anything big enough for you, how many kids you got?" I said. "Four adults, 3 kids, and my wife is pregnant, and I only have $170." He took off his glove and scratched his head and said, "I got a Rambler that I think will seat six, but it's in a snowbank".

When I saw that Rambler get towed into the shop all covered with snow and rusted out, I thought, "Oh God, where are you?" They swept off the snow and aired up the tires and put in a starter. We loaded our party of seven in that car and it sat so low in the back that I had to crank my neck to see the road otherwise all we could see was the Moon! It was late afternoon by the time we were done. I was tired, and discouraged. We stopped at a Wendy's for food and as I looked at the front of that American Motor Company Rambler, I thought, God, I need a word from you. We're broke. Our loved ones don't support what we're doing, and in my heart I want to just give up and get my well-paying management job back. <u>Who are we anyway???"</u> God guided my gaze to the grill of that overloaded, rotted out Rambler. I glanced at the front grill on the car where it gave the model name.

It said, "*AMBASADOR*"! God whispered, "That's who you are!"

Chapter Seventeen

Guns & A Long Awaited Baby

Six shots were fired in rapid succession. A return volley of automatic weapon fire followed it. What ensued was a gal walking around the streets for 2 hours screaming. I went in and peeked at my kids...all peacefully asleep on their sleeping bags. Mandy was peacefully asleep in her Porta-Crib. She was the first natural born Dobbelmann in 3 generations. I went into the tiny living room to cry out to God. It was 5AM. We shared this small 2 bedroom Apartment with another family of four so I tried not to let them hear my tears. All I could see in my mind was the inside of a 727 flying north. Gunfire happened nearly every other night outside our place in San Salvador. The kidnapping and violence got so bad that we had the wives and children stay back at our apartment. I said, God, I thought I had worked through all this back in the states! I knew these countries were at war! And now I want to leave! Can't you understand? It's my instinct as a Dad! Right then God gave me a profound vision. I saw an El Salvadoran man walking among the carnage of his own village after a battle. In my Vision, he found his Daughter that he had waited three generations for...dead.

I realized that as Paul said in Romans 1 *"I am a debtor to the Greek and the Barbarian, the wise and the unwise, (the Guatemalan and El Salvadoran) and I am ready to proclaim the Gospel to them."*

YWAM received a personal invitation from the president of El Salvador to teach in the Cadet Training Program, and provide an hour of religious education in every high school in the country. He actually said to our YWAM director, "we want you to be in charge of all Religious activities of our country! I wonder if he had checked with the Catholics???

Anyway, YWAM had no where near the man-power to even begin to meet this need, but our team was one of the first available to go through this huge open door of opportunity. We would minister to up to a thousand soldiers at a time! Police and others would come up to us on the street and beg us to come to their home to teach them about God. I had never experienced such a sense of destiny in my life. As we would go door-to-door, people would whisper as we talked or prayed because Christians were targets of the Communist Insurgency.

I remember once when we were going door to door and people seemed sort of skittish. They would say things like, "I guess I can take your Bible. Thank you, goodbye". They seemed passionless and very un-engaging...very different from normal Latin Hospitality. Then I arrived at one house and the mother was very quiet as she spoke and she said, "shhh, my daughter is a member of the Communist party. The Communists came through here last month and killed many of my neighbors. That's my Daughter by the sink". She motioned over her shoulder where we could see her daughter washing dishes.

I had a heart-breaking experience at one Military Base. We prepared our Drama characters and sound system as I noticed helicopters coming and going. Bodies would get unloaded that were blown apart or missing arms or legs. Men would wheel themselves out in wheel chairs with bloody bandages wrapped around them or around missing appendages. After we finished our performance, Ellie and I would go out and talk to the soldiers personally. My son Chris who was now seven said, "Dad, ask that soldier how old he is". I did…he was 13! I asked others. Many were 13, 14, and 15 years of age. Outfitted with grenades, guns, bullets, and all the military stuff. I prayed with one and turned around to greet another and saw that he was playing with my 13 month-old daughter. Amanda would climb up on the concrete stage we used for our presentation and then run off and he would catch her and swing her around. Then he would put her down and she would crawl up the stairs and do it again. I observed this joyful behavior, and then after the 19-year old soldier swung her around, he just held her at arm's length, starred at her and began to cry as he hugged her. I asked him what was wrong. He said, "I have a daughter about this old. The last time I was on leave, my Wife said, 'I don't want to see you again until the War is over, and I don't want our Daughter to see you. It's just too hard thinking you might die'"

We ministered in villages that were almost only women, children, and old men. All the young men had been killed. We ministered in areas where the earthquake had destroyed nearly everything. The Evangelical church responded with great sacrifice in Guatemala after these tragedies. They dug bodies out of rubble, they comforted the hurting, they provided for the orphans, they built Health Clinics, and above all, they proclaimed Christ- and Him Crucified. Before the Earthquake and the War, Guatemala was less that 4% Evangelical. Now it is nearly

40%. It was a great privilege to be part of this mighty move of God, and the sacrifice was nothing compared to the sacrifice made by the Savior for us.

One of the ways that God makes us a more powerful Autograph is through harsh or insensitive leaders. You can expect that to happen in your life, but if you have a biblical attitude, it will benefit you so much! Our leaders while we were in El Salvador were this way. Oh, they had many good qualities! Saul in the Bible had many good qualities; he was anointed by God, but his bad quality sure made life tough for David.

Much can be learned by observing the behavior of the three Leader Kings of Israel: Saul, David, and Absalom. The Bible records it just like it is. Leaders are a combination of God's Glory, and their own "warts". Ellie and I are stronger and wiser because we chose to submit to them. They built faith bridges that we have walked on. We owe much of what we are to these leaders.

God had given both Ellie and I a word before we left on our El Salvador Ministry. My word was "Honor" and her word was "Embrace". She embraced the impersonal and even legalistic leadership style of her leader and I honored her Leader's Husband who was my leader. God did not permit me to gossip about him even though he was very insensitive to my position as a Dad and Husband. God would lead me to scriptures like Matthew 18 and a few times I had a personal audience as we were back from outreach and usually shirtless for the great heat. There is a biblical way to appeal to authority, and by God's Grace I did that. The main thing is to always want what's best for them and to never dishonor them.

Sandy would go after Ellie's self-pity in the impersonal way of leaving notes delineating her problems, but because of Ellie's embracing heart, she walked that "Faith Bridge" to freedom from self-pity. We all developed a friendship that transcended those times.

We also developed the insight that while we are "in battle" we do not have the luxury of bringing up disagreements. Submission is the key. You must believe that God will work through your leader or husband or parent. Later, when the storm is done, address personal problems alone with that person, without ever gossiping, and only when we are <u>not</u> engaged in important things like an outreach, ministry, church service, or about to have important fellowship with others.

If you develop this discipline in your life, you become a trusted Ally by Christ. Develop it not, and you will remain a mere man or woman that Christ cannot trust to lead. In fact, if you lack self control, He can't even trust you to follow!

Whenever we would return to the States, we would show up at churches in our faithful Rambler Ambassador with a car top carrier and our 4 kids. I would preach, show pictures, and tell incredible stories of high adventure. Oh, I had to put some used station wagon springs in it to carry the load of our family. They jacked up the rear end of that car nicely! I never had to look at the stars when I drove it after that. Whenever I preached, I would give a challenge at the end of the service like, "who will go wherever God wants, whenever He directs you, and at whatever personal cost and do whatever He tells you anywhere in the world?" Maybe 10% would raise their hands, but many of those went and changed the world! Others became faithful givers and local workers. We would get some great offerings and we needed them! We had no home, just the car named "Ambassador". YWAM always had a room or two somewhere where we would call home. Ellie would go to a market and get some flowers and some flowered plastic like what is popular in Latin America and use them as table cloths over cardboard boxes and dress up the tables with flowers and make the rooms feel like home. We had wonderful, faithful partners who stood with us in God's work. I remember this precious church in Red Wing. It was called Christian Center. They would always take up the biggest offerings and show us love and bring us out for a great meal. They loved us and they loved our kids. We would go down to the nearby Mississippi River and look at the offering and just weep at God's faithfulness through his "Family".

We saw miracles as well as miraculous provision. Ellie was miraculously healed of Hepatitis. Mike was miraculously healed of Blood Poisoning. The doctor was absolutely amazed. Ellie was having horrible vertigo problems and hearing loss. A surgeon at Oral Roberts "City of Faith" did the surgery for free! We would marvel at how the kid's shoes and clothes never wore out. Mike nearly fell off of a cliff. Someone restrained him as he was falling. Amanda nearly fell out of a second floor window when she was learning to crawl. Below there was nothing but concrete, and her 5 year old brother Tim had the sense to hold unto her.

During our Language studies, many of our teachers came to Christ.

God provided good schooling for our kids, and four of them finished college degrees later in life. This had never happened in all the generations of our family.

Our kids are the ones with stories of faith now! Ellie and I are so proud of them. The Autographer is proud too!

Chapter Eighteen

The Dove Arrives

In the Fall of 1985, YWAM wanted all its Leadership and staff back in Arkansas for what I found out was a major re-alignment of staff. They asked me and Ellie to move to Arkansas and be involved with a program of taking church folks to give out Bibles in other lands. I did not want to do this at all! It was bad enough when they called us back from Guatemala. I was just getting "comfortable" there. Now they wanted us to not return??? It was horrible news. I was introduced to the Director of the program, Clark Barnard. He asked if I wanted to go for a walk and talk. I told him, Clark, I can think of little that I would want to do in the world LESS than stay in Arkansas and work with you". He smiled and said, "Let's go for a walk and see if I can broaden your frame-of-reference". Little did I know this was an entry into a more powerful ministry than this mortal could have ever dreamed of?

During our walk, I told Clark that God gave me a word on the bus when we were returning just the week before. He asked me to tell him what god had said. God had told me, "When you return to Latin America, I want you to bring a hundred more like you with you". I had thought where will I find a hundred like me??? I had made a list as we were just south of Tampico on that bus to see if I could come up with a hundred people. I came up with five and gave up and gave the whole idea to God. Clark said, "Let me give you what might be the strategy to fulfill that call." He talked about serving pastors; and that did become the strategy.

Long story short, since that time I have personally brought over 7000 people to Mexico by Coach Bus on short-term Missions Trips. Those 7000 have won over 100,000 to Christ. It has spanned 25 years. We have seen churches that were ready to die brought into great revival and restoration, we've seen the power of the Holy Spirit descend in parks and streets, we've seen the lame walk, hundreds of gang-members saved and even some whole communities become safe and productive after our work in them-literally, stories of miraculous revival! We've seen some demonically influenced men come with guns and other weapons to kill us; to even run over us with their cars, and they would surrender to Christ. We have rejoiced, danced, and worked side-by-side with these wonderful neighbors to the South. Many of those participants are in full-time ministry today.

This call is what gave birth to Dove International in 1991.

Oh yes, what about the hundred that God said I was supposed to bring with me? The very first of our hundreds of Outreaches was to Hermosillo, Mexico just 5 months after God gave me that word. You know how many were on that outreach? 101!

I wonder who the guy was that disobeyed God?

THREE TITANS!

Three "Titans" that I had the opportunity to work with who changed my life were David Jones (my first pastor), Oren Paris (Director of YWAM Latin America), and Steve Holte (President of Key Ministries). These men built Faith Bridges that no one else could build and I was one of the privileged ones to walk with them. Dove International's success was because these men influenced my life before I built it! These are the men with whom if you fall into a pit with a Lion on a snowy day, they will defeat the Lion and get you out!

They would always look for the way things could be done. They would never just fret over a problem and talk about how it couldn't be done. Naysayers would shout at them and mumble about their mistakes, but while others mumbled, they just kept doing what God called hem to. Did they make mistakes? Well, how about you? Have you? Instead of asking such questions, let's instead learn from their rare and daring Leadership. Before you criticize another's ministry, be sure that you have accomplished more than they! It is always the armchair quarter back who has the luxury to judge rather than achieve.

Maybe Teddy Roosevelt said it best:

> *"It is not the critic who counts; not the man who points out how the strong man stumbles, or where the doer of deeds could have done them better. The credit belongs to the man who is actually in the arena! Whose face is marred by dust and sweat and blood; who strives valiantly; who errs, and who comes short again and again! Know this: There is no effort without error and shortcoming. Let me see the one who will actually strive to <u>do</u> the deeds! Who knows great enthusiasms and great devotions; Who*

spends himself in a worthy cause; Who at the best knows in the end the triumph of high achievement, and who at the worst, if he fails, at least fails while daring greatly! His place shall never be with those cold and timid souls who neither know victory nor defeat."

To be sure, I learned a lot from their mistakes as well. But may their legacy be remembered in honor.

> ***God does not always call the qualified, but He <u>always</u> qualifies the called!***

When one chooses to obey the call to be a Gladiator, God makes sure Heaven's resources are available to him. That man or woman may not take advantage of those resources, but they are there.

I remember a time that God wanted to lead me into some special "qualifying". I had started Dove International and we were beginning to provide good professional transportation of our own as a package deal for individuals to have a "hands on" ministry experience in Mexico. I was driving from one church speaking engagement to another and decided to take a "long-cut" through a scenic area of Wisconsin to get there. It was easy to talk to the Lord and sip my coffee as I traveled. Suddenly God spoke very clearly to me. It was one of those verbal words. He said, "Darrell, I want you to give your heart 100% to the primary thing that I've called you to" I knew what He was talking about. It was Dove International. He wanted me to provide the best Short-Term Missions outreaches in the World! But some things were competing for my heart...Good things actually!

I have always loved being involved in politics and in the pro-life movement. I also love teaching Christians on important life issues and I was even starting a church! I was involved in all these good things, but I knew the primary thing was the bus outreaches to Mexico. I thought, "Wow, I've got to think more about what God is telling me and maybe give up these other time-consuming things. I'll write it in my journal and deal with it later."

I arrived at the church in Hudson, Wisconsin and comfortably greeted the Pastor and a few others and discussed the service schedule. I told him that I'll just sit in the back until its time for me to speak. Suddenly a man with a prophetic gifting stood up and began prophesying to a man in the front row. I thought to myself, "Cool, I always love observing these Prophets". He finished with the man in the front row and his eyes lifted and he began to scan the back of the church. His eyes landed on me and with quite a quick step he made his way back to where I was. He pushed his way into the row in front of me, nearly tripping over people's feet; He stopped right in front of me and said, "Sir, the Lord is telling you that you need to give your heart 100% to the primary thing that He has called you to!" I got goose bumps. God had confirmed His word verbatim to me. I immediately stopped my activities in these other good things and gave myself to the Mexico bus outreaches.

Within 3 years we had 4 more buses. We developed a reputation of having the best Coach Bus Missions ministry there was. Individuals and whole youth groups would come with us year after year.

A short time later, I had another "autograph" moment that rocketed me into greater success. During a prayer time one day, I started feeling sorry for myself. I had teen children and one was causing problems. I said, "God, I wish my father was alive and I could call him and ask what he would do." God spoke to me very firmly, "Darrell, the wound of your Father's death will be with you forever". I responded, "Lord, that's not very nice. It even sounds sort of insensitive!" He then said, "It's a wound that's healed, but it will always be visible and in your memory. You must now stop wanting a dad and start being a dad (spiritual dad) to all these thousands of teens riding the buses with you to Mexico." I literally felt Him writing His Autograph across that wound. It became part of my strength instead of my weakness! Dove International's growth exploded.

God provided new and great staff. We began getting hundreds of repeat customers. Whole youth groups would go each year. Thousands were being won to Christ in Mexico by ordinary lay people, most of them were teenagers. We saw God grip whole communities. Churches with problems were healed and some doubled or tripled in size after we left. I would tell the participants, "just go like Jesus did. Share your personal story about what Jesus did in you. Pray for the sick and comfort the hurting. Go out and love like Jesus did" I remember a rather spiritually shy 16 year old saw a Mexican kid with Polio. His leg was all withered. He took some companions and said, "Darrell said to just pray and love people like Jesus did. Let's pray for him". The boy's leg immediately straightened out and he got up and walked. The kids were beside themselves with joy. Many returned year after year and would say, "Dove outreaches are the most exciting thing I do all year". Teens would tell me, "I feel like a family doing exciting stuff together". My own son Brian set a goal of going to Mexico twice each year.

> *"When one chooses to obey the call to be a Gladiator, God makes sure heaven's resources are available to him."*

Many of the outreaches did not have miracles like the above. Most of the time it was only hundreds getting saved. Thousands of Mexican kids raising their hands to give their lives to Jesus, and God speaking more clearly than ever to the American Teens who were participating.---Oh, is that all?

We would do crazy things like put a devil mask on some kid and another person would put a rope around him like he had him as a prisoner. We would do it just to stir up a crowd. Then we would lead the devil back to a central area and "kill" him and play with the crowd on weather he was really dead or not and the biblical way to subdue the devil. Sometimes we would have three devils and interview them or do some other crazy thing to get a crowd, and then the teens would minister in drama or testimonies and people would come forward wanting to surrender to Jesus; sometimes in tears.

Its been 5 years since the last Outreach, but I still often get someone running up to me at Walmarts or some church somewhere in towns around Minnesota to see if I remember them. They have great stories about the mighty things God did on a Dove trip and then they introduce me to their spouse and say, "Darrell I remembered your teaching on how not to marry a flake and I didn't. Here are my husband/wife/kids.

I hold back tears.

THE GREATEST ENEMY OF THE BEST IS THE BETTER

Whenever God has got something great, the Devil has a "curve ball". There was a good chance that Dove

International may never have happened. In October of 1988, in the years leading up to Dove's birth, I was coming to the tail end of having been sent out from YWAM to Minnesota to work with Minnesota churches to put them on Key Ministries buses and send them to Mexico to be serviced by YWAM in their ministry. It was a very successful year and hundreds of people went but I was feeling like our time was coming to a close in MN. And I was anxious to get back on the field. I got a call during that time from Oren Paris who was the Director of YWAM. He asked me if I was thinking my time was done in Minnesota and if I would like to be the Director of YWAM in Mexico. I told him that my heart is jumping at the idea, but I will pray about it and talk to my Wife. I didn't pray much at all! I thought, "This is what I've been waiting for!" My heart leapt at the idea. I would be international YWAM leader!

In my heart, I was already looking forward to fellowshipping with other leaders and I began dreaming about Mexico!

Oren wanted me to come down and strategize the whole thing. My attitude was, "hey, we'll just move back down right now". I was at the storage agency and setting up a unit we could put all of our stuff in and just deal with it later and the whole family will move to Arkansas before being released to begin our work in Mexico. The lady turned the contract around and set a pen on it for me to sign. The Holy Spirit said, "Don't sign it". I tried to sign it again, and the Holy Spirit said, "Don't sign it! Go now to the Fairgrounds and pray". The lady looked confused at my hesitation. I told her, "Hey, I just thought of something I have to do right now. I'll take care of this later". She said, "ummm, ok".

I went to the fairgrounds and prayed. The Lord laid out this whole new direction. He said, "Darrell, I want you to move to Glenwood and start a Spirit-Filled church." I could show you the place at the Alexandria fairgrounds where he spoke to me. It was that clear.

Ellie prayed and felt confirmed in her heart that this should be our direction

MY WAYS ARE NOT YOUR WAYS

Hey, you Real Estate people, check this out! We moved into the high rent district of Glenwood, Minnesota...ahem, $200./month. The place was rundown. When it rained, it poured in through the garage roof. When we flushed the toilet, it leaked in through the kitchen ceiling. The grass was two feet long and the interior of the house was like a dungeon, but it had a huge living room-perfect for Bible Studies. This is how I started my first Church; with a Home Bible Study, so I wanted to do it again!

We moved our stuff down in an old blue school bus from Key Ministries the day before Thanksgiving, 1988. After I put the mattress in the larger bedroom upstairs, I knelt beside it and cried. I could have been a National Director of YWAM in Mexico and instead I'm setting up our new life in Glenwood, MN. Through my tears I said to God, I don't want to be here. I want to be in Mexico. Mexico City grows by more than the whole population of this town every week!" Then God spoke to my heart, "You're not ready for Mexico." Facetiously I responded, "Am I ready for Glenwood?" You know what he said? Guess!

We started putting together the Bible Study. God even showed me where the church would be built, but for now we met in our home. Ellie led worship with her guitar. People got excited. They wanted me to be pastor, but I couldn't commit since I was doing Mexico Mission Trips. I found a guy to be Pastor and we thought we were on the way, but another leader in the Assemblies of God had come on board with the church planting effort and he had different ideas. He did not want the man I had chosen. I gave it all over to him, so he did the rest of the heavy lifting to make it a church. Now Minnewaska Assembly of God stands as a testament to God's leading.

After we lived in the house for 2 years, I was ready to want to leave again. It was hard in those early days raising money to be missionaries even though our work was flourishing with participants. We were tying thousands into Key Ministries buses, but the buses often were in a poor state of repair and drivers many times left a lot to be desired. YWAM ministry was beckoning to me again.

Then the Lord presented the most audacious idea I ever heard. He told me to buy the house I was renting and He gave me a price I should offer: $10,000! I was kneeling beside my bed before retiring. Ellie was reading in bed. I told God, "Why would I want to buy the house at whatever price! Relationships are strained with Key Ministries, and that price is ridiculously low-they would never accept it". God spoke to my soul, "My ways are not your ways and my thoughts are not your thoughts". I took it as a divine rebuke! I crawled into bed and shared everything with Ellie. Right away she saw what I did not. She said, "Darrell, maybe He's not rebuking you, maybe He's letting you know that things would turn out better than you could ever foresee if you just obey Him". I said, "Oh yeah, I see what you mean. Except how could anything turn out good by buying a house in Glenwood?"

I obeyed God and visited the Realtor with the offer of $10,000. He laid his pen down and said, "Darrell, I know that they will come down on their price, but this is ridiculous". He wrote it up. They turned it down. I took it as just eating too much pizza before going to bed for even getting such a crazy idea.

Eight months later God told me, "Go back and offer them the $10,000. again." I said, "No way God! I'm making a fool out of myself." I met with Les Strecker, the realtor the next day. He said, "Hello Darrell, so, you want to make another offer on the house. How much?" I said, "$10,000." He leaned forward in his chair; laid the pen on the table and said, "Haven't we been down this road?" I appealed to him that I did not want to waste his time nor offend the owners, but that it would be a dream to own the house (I lied). Please offer it one more time." He did. They said, "Yes!"

WASKA WAX & WORKS

There was a short time right before I started "Dove" that things didn't make sense. God had always provided, but now, for the first time I did not have enough money to pay bills. Now I even owned a home! I was trying to be a Missionary to a foreign land while living in Glenwood, MN. I just did not look enough like a real Missionary in that situation

A close friend, Dan Bawinkle, was visiting from Illinois and we were talking about the issue. He was seated and I was leaning against the stove. I was sharing about how we were there in Glenwood and I felt like God had called me there to start a spirit-filled church and now I don't have enough money to live. He looked up at me and said some very prophetic words. "Darrell, God is calling you to start an Auto Detailing Service and it will be very visible work that will convey to the community that you're a hard worker and will dispel some of the mystery around you as this new resident who goes on trips to Mexico."

I brought it before the Lord in prayer because it seemed so crazy. I was offered to do some brick-work in Rochester with another friend; so I was doing that to bring in some extra money. I made up a half-page flyer that read: WASKA WAX AND WORKS Spring Special $60. Ask about our mobile service. Blah Blah. The "Waska" name is popular in the area because of nearby Lake Minnewaska. The flyer was a complete "faith thing" (or maybe it was an outright lie) because I had no business, no spring special, no equipment and no mobile service! I made up those hand bills by faith and they were sitting on my seat as I took off for Rochester one morning. I was just driving out of Glenwood. It was a little before 8AM and the Lord said, "Turn around and go to Steinbring Chevrolet and give them a Waska Wax and Works Advertisement." I said, "I don't want to, I've got my coffee and donut and I've gotta go to Rochester." His response to me was to "turn around and do it right now". I did.

I walked into the dealership and said, "Where's the boss". He was just coming out of a Conference room with his salesmen. I said, "Excuse me sir, I'm the president of Waska Wax and Works and I'd like to interest you in our spring special." His jaw dropped and he said, "You've got to be kidding me. We were just talking about how on earth we are going to get 45 used cars on our back lot ready for sale. When can you start?" I had no equipment, the business was a phantom, I was the president of nothing, and I had no money even to buy equipment. I told him I had some stuff to do and I'd be by at noon to pick up the first car. I hurried to Walmart and cashed a rubber check for a Wet Vac and some supplies. I was hoping I could get paid for the first car and put money in the bank before it cleared the next day. Talk about flying by the seat of your pants! I did the first truck. Everything was thumbs up and I made thousands in supplemental income that first year. My wife and I did all the detailing right on our driveway. I even paid my older kids 50 cents an hour to help (shame on me-that's almost child abuse). I had numerous comments from Passers-by about how hard I work. The prophesy was fulfilled perfectly.

By next year, Dove was up and running and bringing in cash from its Outreach fees, but Waska Wax and Works showed how much God enjoys humor and relationship building as He provides for His children.

God had flawlessly led me through all kinds of briar patches and growing experiences that were necessary before releasing Dove International. I could have never worked this stuff into a "Five year plan". Many times I even felt so unfaithful, even irresponsible, but God was unflinchingly faithful.

Sometimes we are not ready to meet goals-or even make goals! They are for a later walk of faith! Sometimes we are too blinded by pain, dysfunction, or lack of Insight. All we can do is hold on to God as He leads.

I remember a time that I was with my good friend, Clark Barnard. We were in his Toyota driving through the rain to New Orleans to catch a flight to Guatemala. The engine started knocking and "gave up the ghost" about 150 miles from the airport. Some YWAMer from New Orleans came to rescue us. They had a very short tow strap and began to pull me as I drove the Toyota. The blinding rain and foggy windows and following just a few feet from the tow vehicle at highway speeds was terrifying. I honked the horn and put on the brakes to let them know that I just could not do this! Clark took over as he was towed all the rest of the way to N.O. Later I asked him, "How did you get the guts to steer that thing that close to the tow vehicle while being pulled in those horrible conditions?" He said,

"I just looked at his tail lights and <u>trusted</u> he would do the right things while I followed".

Sometimes we must do the same with God. God will build it all into you and lead you through it all to a place where you can make Goals; where you can have Vision. You'll be surprised when people start to listen to your vision and follow you. I was!

It's difficult to articulate Vision when you're blinded by tears, or muffled by your own immaturity. We have to take His hand and seek His face and FOLLOW! If we seek leadership, titles, fame, or money as we seek the Lord, we handicap ourselves! When our needs are great, we are tempted to seek wrong things and even become vulnerable to wrong forms of comfort or companionship. We must just <u>seek the Lord.</u> There will be many tears in the process, but "joy comes in the morning"…and so does success, blessing, honor, and life!

A Disciple is an active student of Christ's. Are you active? Active at following Christ's every move? Active at learning and listening for every word and directive? Active at changing any habit and conforming completely into whatever He wants?

When you relinquish the Painter's Brush to the Painter, He is finally free to create the Masterpiece that you were created to be!

Chapter Nineteen

The Greatest Joy

My wife and I raised teenagers for 20 years and it was one of the greatest joy of our lives! What did you say?

Ok, I confess, there were many times of tears and anger; many times of desperate prayer with my wife, and even sometimes we're tempted to feel hopeless.

Ok, that's true sometimes, but the opportunities afforded by raising teens are a phase of life that is a magnificent opportunity! It will produce rich fruit for all as you push through the barriers to reach new vistas of understanding, wisdom, and relational excellence. This time in life will never come again, so don't just hold your breath and wish for it to end. ENJOY IT! ENJOY IT! ENJOY IT! God won't just teach them. He'll teach you!

Bear with me for just part of a chapter while I "show you the kids"! Then I'll end the book with a couple chapters that will empower and encourage you. If you're raising teens, don't jump over this chapter!

Each of my kids became part of God's rich Autograph on my life. They are "*my heritage and my reward*".

I'm going to do something very dangerous. Actually put in print what I've observed in each of my kids. God help me if I get it wrong!

CHRIS

He is our first born-Married to Amanda Mildred (we call her Millie to distinguish her from our own daughter Amanda). They have three boys and one of our rare grand daughters. Chris has been an example-setter. He has been a model of faith and perseverance for the other kids to see.

He has struggled greatly with doubt as a Teen and sometimes even into his thirty's, but has always tempered that with a determination that if God is real, by golly, he's going to know Him! Through his hard times, he has <u>always</u> come through. He has always been determined to seek truth, work hard, and do right. I ran across his old Oswald Chambers devotional lately that he used in his twenties, and took note of the notes he made. It reaffirmed what I always knew. He is a seeker, and once he discovers the truth, he runs with it. Seeking and yielding to the Truth of God is the key to receiving new Brushstrokes from the Creator. Personal preferences, ego, and the desire to be right all must yield to Truth! He married a gal who embraces this same pilgrimage.

Chris is my firstborn. He absorbed all our mistakes as we learned to be parents and he still loves us! Burned into my memory are his early antics, his 5 year-old hands full of grease as we replaced a motor in the 54 Chrysler Wagon, our 1st mission trip together to Mexico, and the first time he hoisted a canoe over his head in the Boundary Waters Canoe Area.

Hey Dad's! Firstborns need <u>more</u> of your time! There is nothing wrong with your other kids noticing that you spend some extra time with your Firstborn! Look up

Firstborns in the Bible and get advice from it. Do special projects and go places with them alone. It's not too late! Pray about what to do and just do it now!

Chris rose above and defeated many of the Generational weakness in our family lines. Years ago, when he was a teen, God told me that he would do this.

He attended YWAM in LA and then a subsequent Cross-cultural school in the Dominican. He got a 4-year Cross-cultural degree at NCU. He spent a couple of months in Morocco living with Muslim families determined to learn how to reach them. He met Millie as they both pursued Cross-cultural studies at NCU. Virtually on the heels of the completion of their ministry training, they were married and got into kid raising mode.

Chris began his career in ministry at Teen Challenge as one of the organizations' auto mechanics and later moved to broaden his proficiency (and make more money) as an Auto Technician and now works for Weinhagen's in St. Paul.

TIM
Tim is the one who brought music to the highest level of any in our family. Although Ellie is still the most prolific Song Writer, Tim and Amanda brought performance and presentation to a new level in our family. Though all of our kids led & loved worship, it was him and Amanda that made a living off of it. Tim had one song that even went international on the Vineyard Label. I remember when Tim discovered music in his own genes. He got sort of tied into a rocky Christian radio station that I wasn't too sure about, but then exploded from there! He attended YWAM training in Chico, CA. where he met the love of His life. He is married to a former YWAM leader, Noreen and they have 2 boys and a girl and live in Perth, Australia where her family lives. We miss them all deeply.

Second Borns are natural competitors. Most of the daring fighter pilots during WW2 were Second Borns. Tim was always too loving to crush someone in competition. He has a very competitive spirit, but probably the greatest Self-control of any man in the world; and his ethics always would allow others to win if he thought it would help them. He had a tremendous ability to resolve his own anger quickly for the sake of others. What a quality! Tim's caring nature made his competitive and independent side...cooperative! He was an inspiring leader in music; in High School he would gather all of our folding chairs and bring them to the park for these well-attended worship sessions with his peers. The chairs always got destroyed, but I figured it was a good trade-off!

The Band he was in, "All Weather Human" held the honor of being the most in-demand Christian group in the upper-Midwest.

Tim has always loved life, loved Jesus, embraced purity, and been the most uncomplicated of all of us. He could always find great joy with life and with friends. His tender smile and encouraging nature gives you life by just being near him. I've often thought of getting some WWTD Bracelets. You can guess what the "T" stands for. Whenever I'm tempted with anger, it would help me! "How would Tim behave right now?" Tim earns a living with his Painting Business in Perth and leads others to God in Worship every opportunity he gets.

MIKE
Mike is the only of my kids for whom God gave me a verbal promise the night he was born. He let me know that his life was so important to God that the devil would try to take him out. Try to take him out he has! He nearly drowned, he nearly died of blood poisoning and God

miraculously healed him, to the amazement of the Doctor. He nearly fell off of a cliff in Mexico. A friend grabbed his hand just in time. During some silly times as a teenager, he had other bouts with near-death moments. The Devil has used bad friends for years to nearly destroy him, but he finally rose above all of that and was gloriously saved while in jail! After that His heart became tender; even his eyes became soft; his heart of mercy and service led him to stand by others who could not help themselves. He went to YWAM Seattle and then on to get a Psychology degree at NCU.

How can I forget his learning to ride a bike at Lake Geneva Bible Camp; and his little tummy always sticking out under the hem of his shirt when he was 4 and 5 years old. All the times when he would look up at me with his deep Blue Eyes after he did something wrong.

When Ellie discovered she was pregnant with him, times were financially tight. The doctor asked, "Do you want to keep it..?" When I held him in my arms and now when I look at the man he is today, and when I look at his two sweet kids, I think what kind of a society and what kind of a Physician would encourage a Mom to deprive her offspring of life? Thank God that His Word and His spirit gave us better council

I've heard that 3rd Borns can be more easy-going. They don't worry as much. Mike definitely had an easy going side, but had a bad habit of latching unto easy-going <u>bad</u> friends. I definitely should have "rescued" him a couple of those times! I had a mis-defined view of ministry where I thought we were going to make a difference in that bad friend's life. Thankfully, he emerged from this great amount of destruction with his own Autograph from God

I discovered one of his old suitcases recently while cleaning. In it were items that transitioned his bad and good years. It's a thrill to compare his final high school year with his first year in college. Everything changed from "D's" to "A's. From criminal activity to benevolent mercy. From helpless bondage to hope-filled friendships.

After he surrendered to Christ he started hanging with great people at YWAM and at NCU. He even attended our Discipleship school in Guatemala. He started an era of achievement which lasts to this day. He has a 4-year Psychology degree from NCU where he met the Christian gal he wed: Andrea. He had a vision to ride across the States by bicycle and that desire developed into a Bike Ministry called "Venture" that has raised thousands of dollars for other ministries and has crossed foreign continents by peddle power. I remember one year he had put nearly 10,000 miles on his bicycle! I told him, "A lot of people don't even do that in their car.

He was a Regional Manager for Jamba Juice in Mpls., and just recently surprised us be quitting that and getting into management for Chick-Fil-A of which he raves about their business and marketing principles.

AMANDA
Our only daughter! The Girl that the Dobblemann family waited 3 generations for. My dad had no sisters, I had no sisters (until after my dad died and I got half sisters), my Brother got married and had four boys and I think gave up trying for a girl. Then I got married and had three boys, and then…Amanda was born. We didn't even have a girl's name picked out! Since her birth, there has been one other female born into the extended Dobbelmann family, the daughter of my brother Dave…Diedra.

Daughters occupy the most special place of all people in the hearts of their fathers! You daughters who think you're not important to your dads are lied to by the devil. You're mistaking their personality or temperament for a lack of love! Just assume they love you and whisper words of respect in they're ear. They'll soften!

This dad was no different. I loved to carry her when she was a baby and talk endlessly to her. I would sing her songs and pray with her as we walked on our roof-top that overlooked the volcanoes in Guatemala. When she was little and we had Outreach Teams, she would come into the Men's dorm sometimes and sleep with me. It was so cute. I remember once when she was real little, she fell asleep on top of my chest. When we turned the lights off, the other guys were still taking flash pictures in the dark, because it was so cute.

Amanda was a true joy as a child and a "dream teenager" to raise. She just loved life, loved family, loved friends, and loved God. She found no reason to act out! She loved mimicking her mom and like all little girls, after she accomplished something, she would look up at her folks with those cute Green Eyes as if to say, "Am I pleasing you?"

In her senior year of high school, things changed. She became very focused on Achievement. To me, she had always achieved, but in her senior year she felt she needed to be more serious. Thankfully she emerged and became liberated from some of the "control" issues that led to an eating disorder. She studied Music and Worship, has cut three albums, has been a music pastor and now teaches music in LA. She also has a very successful and developing writing career. She finished a 4-year Music degree at NCU with an emphasis on worship.

God has done great things in her faith, in her love for God, and in her relationships. Her wisdom of life grew tremendously after dealing with a string of painful disappointments with life and relationships. The difference is that now she has received a deeper "Autographing" of God. The astounding insight she has acquired has deepened her and given birth to her Writing Ministry. Some of her Blogs on Women's Issues get thousands of hits from all over the world. Check out her writing at www.forteebello.com and check out her music at www.mandydmusic.com

Wisdom is the gift of God for determining to do right in the face of obstacles and adversity. Through the blurred vision of the tears, God creates a confidence of soul, clarity of mind, and compassion of heart that changes even the destiny of others. These are all Brushstrokes that Mandy has personally experienced in recent years.

BRIAN

My wife's concern and even fear came through in her voice, "Darrell, I think I'm pregnant! I missed my time of month" These were the words she shared over the pay phone with me in April of 1992 when I phoned her from Laredo Texas before entering Mexico with still another group of people on the Easter Outreach. A sudden fear struck me too! I thought, "Am I ready to start kid raising all over again at the age of 43, and my wife at nearly 40? I mean, the diapers, the nurturing, the 18 years of training, sports, report cards...yikes!

Well, she <u>was</u> pregnant and on November 14, our 5th child was born, another boy! When I called Mandy from the hospital she said, "What is it?" I said, "It's a boy, honey", there was silence, and she finally said, "Well, at least he's younger than me". We named him Brian which means strength and honor. He has lived up to his name!

Brian has been the greatest blessing of our older parenting years. His strength has never wavered and the honor he has shown his parents has been our mainstay. He has been more than a son. He has a spirit of Protection for his parents and a deep family identity.

He lives just 30 minutes north of us, and it is such a blessing having four of our Grandsons so near.

He always wanted to catch up with his three older Brothers in every way. Well, at this writing I think he has achieved it! He's 23, married with four children-all boys! His confidence and wisdom make up for his oft impatience. His wife, Ariel is a gently, beautiful, and smart young lady who, even though so young, took to mothering like she was born for it!

He managed to squeeze in a 2-year Mechatronics degree at Alexandria Technical College in the midst of raising kids which landed him a great job as an Electronic Assembler at a Custom Machine Business.

Ellie and I have made so many mistakes in raising kids and attribute their wonderful natures more to God's grace than our parenting. I'm serious! There is however, a **sacred trio** of things I would recommend to any parent of teens because if these are not there, it can mess up your best designs for your kids. If they are not there, they can fowl up even those of you who have far better parenting skills than we had. May I share them?

THE SACRED TRIO:

1. **Be "Real" with them.** Never replace a real relationship with Jesus for mere religious behavior! We can all fall into this. We can go to church for the

sake of guilt. We can govern our home out of fear! We can live our doctrines out of pride! We can do good things for the sake of image! Though we will never be perfect, we must be Genuine! The only part of you that will change your kid's lives even after you die is the realness of your faith.

2. **Be There for them.** Always be approach-able. Be a listener! How ironic that in this age of all kinds of communication devices, we can't find someone to listen! In Titus 2 we see that the older women are supposed to teach the younger women how to be a friend to men and to teens! That's what the word "love" means there. It comes from the Greek word "Phileo" which means "Brotherly Love". Philadelphia means "the city of brotherly love. It means be a buddy to your kids as well as be a parent! Buddies don't lecture, pontificate, or condescend. Neither do they ignore them. (By the way Ladies, this is the same way you are supposed to love your Husbands. It's a forgotten art, and if you get it learned, <u>please</u> teach it to others! Men and teens are desperate for it.) Learn to be honestly interested in stuff you're not interested in! Don't just act interested; <u>be interested.</u> Listen to their heart! If you don't, they'll find someone who will!

3. **Trust them.** Yes, even if you find out later that they lied and took advantage of you, and were not "real" in return. Now, I'll admit that with most of my five kids, I had to condition that trust if I found out they were lying. But I still did not do things like snoop around their rooms, and if I humiliated them in front of their friends, I would apologize to them and their friends. Jesus taught us to be faithful and true even when wronged. This is Jesus example to us. He trusts us to be Lights to the world, Salt of the

Earth, and Pillars of Truth even when we fail. Can we do less for our kids?

May I add a 4th thing to the "Sacred Trio"? This is foundational to raising kids of any age. Here it is:

<u>Prioritize your marriage over your parenting.</u>

Often when a marriage hits a snag, one's sense of identity can be more easily found in raising kids, and that takes the primary emphasis. As noble as this seems, you're setting your parenting up for failure, and you're setting up your marriage for some hard times once those kids leave the home. The most secure thing you can do for your kids is to prioritize your marriage. Model a great marriage so that they grow up confident of what a marriage can be. Your kids have to see your love, kisses, hugs, special times, and laughter!

Try not to argue in front of the kids. Especially with a raised voice. Pray for Grace! Don't ever let the kids pit you against each other. Have a united front, and if push comes to shove, moms must differ to the dad's leadership and then settle the difference later - <u>away</u> from the kid's ears! Kid's need to see resolution of conflict; so if you make a mistake, let them see you resolve it...especially if it involves a hug and a smile!

I'm so everlastingly grateful for my wife who has chosen to put God first, and therefore has had the Grace to stand by God, Goodness, and even ... me!

Ok, let me bless you all!

May all the promises of God for your kids be realized! May you enjoy them and they would be your *"joy and your glory"*. May they *"rise up and call you blessed"*! May they be *"fruitful vines that grace your house"*! May you and your kids be yielded as the "Canvases of God" during these few years that you share the same home. May you all enjoy the very Hand of God putting His Brushstrokes upon those Canvases.

Chapter Twenty

The Oasis

"Well guys, its time to leave this little part of Heaven!" said Tom facetiously as we left another Zero Star Hotel in an outback part of India. We have stayed umpteenth million times in the best Zero Star hotels in India as we drill wells and do outdoor crusades in distant rural areas of India. To be sure, many proprietors do their best to clean their establishments, but if you believe a rat or lizard might be your dead Grandma, you just let it run around!

Tom Elie was a great friend who had also been a founding Board Member of Dove International and accompanied me many times with his Church members to evangelize in Mexico. He started Oasis World Ministries in 1996, quit his church of 20 years and asked me numerous times to accompany him to India. In 2007 I met him at a Pastor's conference and said, "Hey Tom, why don't you ever invite me to India any more?" He said, "Because you never come!" I told him, I think that's about to change". This meeting turned out to be a life-changer. Oasis had a vision of seeing 1,000,000 decisions for Christ by the end of 2010. The strategy to accomplish this was:

        Proclaiming the Gospel where it had never been proclaimed in rural areas of India

        Drilling wells in communities in India that had no clean water

Doing Pastor's Conferences in areas where Pastors had little former training.

Building churches in villages that have no church building

Funding national Evangelists in India to do Festivals and equip the churches in Personal Evangelism.

God finally gave me the green light right there at that meeting; so in the Fall of 2007, this Latin America Missionary went to India.

It was a life-changing experience to be sure. Dedicating wells in villages was an "Apostolic" experience! Hindus, Muslims, surround you, many to hear about Jesus for the first time! People are miraculously healed. People weep as they see the love of God and the love of His people, and many many surrender their lives "to the One True God!" Tom let me preach at one of the crusade nights. Nearly 1000 people gave their lives to Christ at one Altar Call! People with totally deaf ears heard and blind eyes saw. Incredible experiences.

As I arrived home with a combination of jet-lag and joy, I thought to myself, "great experience", and I began to prepare to get back to my normal life of Latin American ministry. I began my drive up Interstate 94 to go home and God said to me, "Darrell, I've given you 100,000 souls in Mexico. I'm going to give you 100,000 more in India". What? I dismissed that "Word from God" as jet lag!

The year was 2007 and to be sure our work in Mexico was hitting some difficulties with the growing drug-violence there. Over the next few years it got very serious as the ugly Drug-Cartel violence reached the "borders" in the form of bullet-riddled bodies and scary messages to other Cartels written in blood. Two police chiefs in Laredo Texas were murdered. The second, when he took a hard stand against the Cartels after the death of the first and he was dead within a week! Fewer and fewer people were signing up for our Outreaches and we were having to have them sign scary "release forms" with things like making the parents responsible for the return of the body if their kid should happen to die on the outreach! What parent in their right mind will sign that and then send their kid off with a kiss and a prayer?

SOMETHING NEW

I prayed and God told me, "Darrell, I'm going to bring you into something new" I thought, "oh, oh here it comes; another big move for me and Ellie". Every time in the past that God told us this and once the details came through, it always meant a big move! God said, "No, this new thing will not involve a move". I argued with God, "Lord, I love the Mexico outreaches, lives are being changed; I really love it! I have the busses, I have the facility, I have the staff, and it's effective and powerful...please? Can't you take away the violence in Mexico and let us just continue?" He responded, "The Mexico outreaches will be fewer and fewer and soon they will cease".

At that time I was doing more and more teaching in Youth With A Mission training schools. One day in the spring of 2008 I was working on some Training Manuals and getting frustrated with how they were not coming together. I decided to go to a Pastor's conference in Saint Cloud, MN. As I was driving there, I was thinking about two things; 1) The training manuals, and 2) The "new thing" that God said I would get into. After all, it had been a few months and God was not giving insight. I arrived at the conference and it was laid out beautifully at Jubilee Worship Center with a breakfast, fellowship, and followed by a ministry time to us from a "Prophet". The Prophet stood up and began prophesying to a person sitting in the front row. Then he looked back as though looking for me. I thought, "Wow, here we go again, just like the church in Wisconsin years before". He came right back toward me. I had not talked to him and he knew nothing about my situation. He pointed his finger at me and said, "God wants you to know that these Training Manuals will take care of themselves. You don't need to worry about them anymore". I got goose bumps. Then he said, "And this new thing that God is leading you into..." I thought he's hitting it right on the head right down to the terminology! He continued, "...this new thing that God is leading you into will involve many in the market place, businesses will be involved, and you will have great success". I was excited, but a little deflated. He gave no direction about what it was to be, only those who <u>should</u> be involved...besides, I knew no Businessmen??

    The next day I phoned Tom Elie, because I felt like maybe the word that God spoke to me in the car really was from God and maybe India will be the "new thing". I told Tom about the "market place and Businessmen" thing. He said, "Well, do you know any Businessmen or people with 'deep pockets?'" I said, "I know a Veterinarian in Cokato and a Turkey Farmer in Painesville". He replied, "How about up where you live?" "Well, I know the Banker who gave me a loan for our property and the guy who sold us Bus Insurance, and I do have a buddy who was in the Telephone Business. He said, "I'll come up tomorrow and we'll talk to them".

    The next day we met with the Banker who pledged an initial $1000. and then backed off after he talked to his Dad who owned the bank. Then we drove to Alexandria and met with my Bus Insurance guy, Gordy Billmark. We showed him a video of our work in India and God gripped his heart. He immediately had his secretary write out a check for $1000. and shared a vision. He said, "Here's the first thousand you need, now let's believe God for 30 more area Businessmen to cut you a check for a thousand and you'll have the budget met." He then pulled up his Database and started writing down names of areas Business men he knew would love the project. As I visited these Contacts, God grabbed the heart of one man after another and each of them added more to the list. This was it! The next few weeks God brought together $30,000. And I was introduced to many new Businessmen. There were some with "deep pockets, and some not so deep, but all united together and my ministry partner team came together in just a matter of weeks.

Alexandria Minnesota should be the nerve center of the world for learning what a Christian business community should look like. I met Vern and Paul Anderson of Douglas Machine. I met Tom Schabel of Alexandria Extrusion; I met Tim and Terry Ferguson of Ferguson Brothers Excavating, and Brent Smith of Aagard Corp. These people became my "Steering Committee" along with Gordy to this day. These men have empowered a whole new era of my life and together have raised beyond a quarter million dollars over the years to finance the ongoing and growing vision that is changing nations. Over the intervening years they have been faithful partners of prayer, council, and financial support. Now there are wells in rural areas of India, pastors trained, churches built, and thousands added to the Kingdom of God in India, Guatemala, Nicaragua, Peru, and other Nations because of that one morning I chose to go to the Pastors Breakfast.

One of the great joys of these men is the practical council they give and the accountability they represent. I even asked Paul Anderson to be a spiritual father to me. Men, it is worth being transparent to trusted friends and also an older man and giving him the right to speak into your life. Too many of us are like spiritual orphans just trying to prove ourselves to God and others. I pray that you will find trust relationships as I have. Life is too lonely without them! Christ's autographing cannot be complete without them.

I must stop and thank God for my dear friend and covenant brother, Tom Elie. I would guess that you could find people who have worked for both of us who might say that we are too hard-driving. I have had many ask me, "How can two guys like you be so close. Don't you get irritated with each other? The answer to that is probably "yes"...but you'll have to ask Tom!

The key to our relationship is that each of us sincerely loves souls more than we love our personal preferences. We differ often, but when we discuss our differences, we arrive at which opinion is most important for souls and that's the one we go with. Seek friendships and marriage partners with whom you can have this type of relationship.

Unless you've found something to live for more passionately than your opinion, you'll never have the joy of unity with anyone. Common values must govern the focus of our lives and give us Identity. If our Identity is found in what we think we know, rather than the pursuit to always know more, we will be unteachable and insecure. Finding our identity in our own "death to self" is one of the great and wonderful paradoxes of the Christian life! Jesus said in Mark 8:35 *"If you find your life you will loose it, if you lose your life for my sake and the Gospels, you will save it"*.

Check out my wife's book *"The Small Book of Amazing Paradoxes."* This Great Paradox along with many others are included in it!

I don't think I've ever lived in such an insecure, intolerant, and divided time. People have made a "science" out of Offense! People's egos are built on the fragile and ethereal foundation of personalized truth and when they perceive that you don't put merit in it, they become irate. Identity is a very illusive thing until we find it outside of ourselves! The pursuit to discover those truths will form our new identity. May God help us to regain the great high ground of living our lives and governing our relationships with Truths that come from outside of ourselves! This is where permanence and stability is found and values can be based on more than feelings. Once you find those values, live by them no matter what you're feeling.

May your life prosper as <u>you</u> find Identity not only in the discovery of them, but even in the pursuit of them! This is where Christ can take out His Pen and begin to really give you clarity of thinking, and confidence from your core! This is where you are "Autographed" deep inside! Then you can end the lonely and agonizing pursuit for your identity. You can find it! No more veneers! No more cover-ups hoping that people will discover things you are ashamed of. You can truly become Autographed by a hand far more skilled than your own!

> *"Finding our identity in our own "death to self" is one of the great and wonderful paradoxes of the Christian life"*

My work continues with Oasis to this day as we build our "5 Star Evangelism" Program into Churches of Nations all over the world. We have trained thousands and thousands of Pastors all over the world in this program that inspires them with the power and responsibility of Personal Evangelism! Included in the training is the practical Faith-sharing tool, "The One Minute Witness". Finally we have a faith sharing tool that empowers every Believer how to share their personal story about Jesus and do it with compassion and confidence. Hundreds of thousands are coming to Christ. Whole nations are being changed and challenged.

Gods leading and faithfulness awes me! God's leading on my life has been flawless! If not for Oasis coming at this perfect time in my life, I could have been all dressed up and no where to go! I could have never planned this! God seems to have brought along my previous "Autographing" to prepare me for this moment in my life!

Churches are exploding in size in the nations we work in as the simple and most foundational part of the Great Commission is being reapplied to Christian life – "witnessing". As we become more and more proficient at sharing our faith, it becomes like a "New Normal" for church life. Rather than "going witnessing," we become "witnesses going". We are available to God every day to let the Holy Spirit begin a new friendly conversation. Lost sheep are being led to the Shepherd who died for them. Now they are found! Now they are saved. Now they are where they should be!

Go ahead and say it! "I am a witness of Christ's work in me!"

Go ahead and pray it! "Lord, I'm available today to touch a life with your love!"

Chapter Twenty One

Celebrating

The "Wayward Son" had been with Prostitutes and alcohol for many months. It pained his family's heart greatly. Day after day they offered prayers to God that he would be kept safe and alive and come home. The very real fear that they would be attending this young Son's Funeral was something they always had to try to keep at bay, because they knew they had to live their own lives too. But they loved him and wanted to hold him and have him be part of family fellowship again. Would he ever come to his senses? This man was being autographed by the wrong Father!

Then came the day when the greatest longing of their heart was realized. The son was seen a long way from the front gate of the house and was bowed down in the road praying and weeping. His father was notified that a man resembling his Son was a ways down the road to the house. With great anticipation he went to the front gate and looked down the road. Yes, he was sure it was his son. His clothes were dirty and tattered. His unkempt hair and growing beard made him doubt for a moment, but, yes, this was him. "Oh God, please have this be him" he muttered in prayer. He ran to meet him, but as he ran, the man's boney frame made him doubt again, but when he looked up, the

Dad knew, "this is my Son". He's come home. They embraced and wept in each others arms. Forming words through his tears, the prodigal son said, "Father, I'm not even worthy to be called your son. I have sinned against heaven and against you. Would you make me one of your hired men? If not, I understand and I will go."

The father replied, "Walk back to the house with me my son", and he quickly ordered the servants to bring the best robe into the room, and get some sandals for this poor man's feet. Oh yes, and bring my family ring sitting on my desk. They hurried with his orders. They returned and covered this man's shame with fine clothes. "Now, kill that quality calf that we've been fattening up and plan for a feast and the celebration of all celebrations! This son of mine was dead and now he's alive!" Celebrating is built into the DNA of Human Beings. Cultures all over the world have their forms and expressions of celebrating.

        We celebrate Marriages
        We celebrate the win of our Sports Teams
        We celebrate Graduations & Birthdays
        We celebrate Victory in War
        We even celebrate the Winner of a frog jumping contest!

How can we contain ourselves? Let's celebrate those who finally abandon their prodigal and wayward life & come home to embrace Salvation, Truth, their Father in Heaven!

Celebrating is associated with Salvation in the Bible. The angels rejoice! Notice the Bible never says they rejoice when you get a new church built, or even when you preach a good sermon! But they do rejoice when even just one soul comes to Christ. OK, I celebrated when Dove International got its beautiful property and I think God smiles when I preach a good sermon; but I wonder how many things angels yawn at until a Soul gets saved. Then they stand up and celebrate with God!

Should not the thing that makes Heaven happy make us happy? Paul looked at those who he won to Christ and said, "You are my crown of rejoicing!"

It does make sense that God would reserve a special crown for those who choose to obey His final words: "Be witnesses unto me"

On Judgment Day when God rewards us for our work on the earth and puts us each in the many places where we will rule and reign with him, he also puts crowns on our head.

Here are five of scriptures' crowns:

1 - <u>CROWN OF RIGHTEOUSNESS</u> — Those who love the Lord's appearing
    2 Timothy 4:8
2 - <u>INCORRUPTIBLE CROWN</u>— Those who discipline their bodies and develop
    self control- 1 Cor 9:25-27 -
3 - <u>CROWN OR LIFE</u>— Those who endure patiently through trials
    James 1:12, Rev. 2:10
4 - <u>CROWN OF GLORY</u>— Godly leaders who were examples to their flocks
    1 Peter 5:2-4
5 - <u>CROWN OF REJOICING</u>— The Soul Winner's crown. 1 Thess 2:19, Dan 12:3

Celebration always accompanies the salvation of everyone who is saved. The Bible says that the Angels are intrigued and stand in awe of it! That we as hopelessly fallen physical beings could actually be saved...! Wow!

They stand in awe of the greatness of God in being able to accomplish such a thing! Applause and joyous celebration fills Heaven as the Angels look down from Heaven's portals.

In agony while the Garden of Gethsemane, Jesus strengthened Himself with one thing-that people would finally be free. On the way to the cross, Jesus looked forward to *"the joy that was set before Him"*. The thought of men and women finally having a way of salvation helped him to *"endure the cross; despising its shame"*. The Greatest Time of Heaven's and Earth's Celebration was about to happen!

On the great day of the Wedding Feast of the Lamb, I believe their will be great feasting and celebrating over the souls we have "snatched from the fire" and brought to heaven with us!

Our "renewed minds" will have a new Celestial and even God-like awareness of the multitude of Souls we have won to Christ. God is so pleased when He sees us "polishing our tools" of personal faith-sharing. What better thing can there be than to get really good at sharing how Jesus has touched our Life? I truly believe in that moment after we die, that *"corruption will put on incorruption, mortality will put on Immortality, and we shall see Him as He is"* Wow! Wow! Wow! The Bible says, *"We will know even as we have been known."* <u>We</u> will have an awareness of not only those we have won, but those <u>they</u> have won! The multiplied multitudes of the ones we won and the ones they won become **our** crown of rejoicing that Redeemed People and Angles will celebrate together! I can't wait for that day. I can't wait!

The "ripple effects" of those won by those we have won on earth whom we never could know will be known on that day! Those "ripples" will be the faces of thousands that have been touched by our witness. It will have flowed into other cultures, ages, families, faces, and nations. We will hear the words, *"well done good and faithful servant, enter into the **Joy** of the Lord."*

This is what Jesus' Mission is all about! The question is, will we join Him in it? His mission was to *"seek and to save that which was lost"*. And now we are part of the great "co-mission" We do it together with Him! This is the primary job of the Holy Spirit on earth. To "give us power to be witnesses" Acts 1:8. These were the last words of Jesus before He Ascended Bodily into Heaven. And in Luke 21, He said He will return when the job is done, and only He knows when it will be done to His satisfaction. Maybe you will win the last one to Christ before it's done, and then, all of a sudden, He returns and everything changes.

The Lord will come when the Bride of Christ *"has made herself ready"*. Are we ready? Statistics would seem to say otherwise! Life-Way Research reports that 97% of believers never share their faith with anyone…ever! Ouch! Why are we even here? A better question is "what are we waiting for?"

This is an Emergency!

All Christ's leaders need to huddle right now! How are we going to turn that statistic around? And should there be anything more important and immediate on our "To Do List"?

Personal Evangelism must become the "New Normal" of every believer and every church! In Joy Dawson's words, "There are no boundaries, exceptions, or limitations to the Great Commission"! She also said, "Real fishermen are never content with nibbles". The purpose of fishing is to reel them in! Oh yes, we may spend some time just "sowing worms into the lake", but at some point we get tired of it and need to change our technique or change our location! Every Believer needs to improve his proficiency to where he is leading people to Christ and every leader needs to embrace responsibility for helping them do it!

Actually, let's soften this term, "Personal Evangelism", which is scary to many. Understandably so! It can conjure the idea of "white knuckled" evangelism where we are forcing ourselves to preach at people. Let me set you at ease! Put your preaching finger in your pocket. Get rid of all the fears defined by all the "shoulds". Forget the stereotypical image of preaching to some trapped individual who can't wait to get out of there! We are actually learning how to build new friendships!

Picture a situation:
    Where people are giving you permission to share your personal testimony with them.
    Where you are building a friendship with your testimony and meeting a new person and finding a new friend.
    Where they are not looking at their watch, or thinking your nuts, but they are interested in what you are saying.

This is the picture of the biblical witness.

Friendship must be prioritized and homes must be opened to hospitality for new "infants" in Christ. Then these new believers join you as a friend in church to become part of the fabric of fellowship; and you become a fun friend (not a pious Pharisee).

For the last 3 years, I've been traveling the world and training thousands of pastors with a solution-the 5 Star Evangelism Seminars! Here we train key Pastors and Leaders to be trainers of other trainers. Check out the website for testimonies and even a taste of the Training: www.Oasisworldministries.org

This seminar is a vehicle for the training of our "One Minute Witness" tool that was given to Evangelist Tom Elie nine years ago. Can you articulate your personal story with compassion, clarity, and brevity? Do you want to? I bet you do! You want to be part of the solution to that "emergency statistic" of only 3 % of people sharing their Faith. Together, we're going to bump that up to 3%...10%...or...50%. Imagine what that would do. Millions would come to Christ! Our churches would go to double and triple services.

Let's get about it right now. Let's "redeem the time". Go to www.OneMinuteWitness.org and find the template and add your personal information into it. If you can find someone else to do it with; a partner is always good. Then, go out and try it. Then, refine it. Then, come back to your house and write it out. Then, memorize it. It's ok if it's a "two-minute witness" at first, but then slowly refine it until it's one minute long. Then, refine it some more until it sounds really personal. You will be radically improving it the first two days all the way up to maybe a month, but after the investment of that time, you will own the most valuable and empowering expression of your life - your clear compassionate confident personal story!

Here are some helpful and practical things that will help you win the battle and become an Everyday Witness:

       Think about making a 21 Day Challenge. Research show that it takes about 21 days to make a new habit. Put a sticky note on your fridge that will remind you every day to share your faith with at least one person.

Use the anointed prayer! Its two words! **"I'm available"**! Pray it often. It's just telling God that you are available to be used by Him to touch a one life that day! Oasis sells wrist bands for a buck that read "One More". I wear mine everyday! In the morning when you're prepping for the day, just tell God "I'm available today to touch a life". Usually when I'm around people who might be someone I should share my Witness with, I pray the prayer and the Holy Spirit will usually lead me to talk to someone. Are you available today? There may be a life that only you can touch today...be available to do it!

Grow in your sensitivity to the Holy Spirit. When it comes to you starting new Faith relationships, He is your Friend! He is the Pro of Pro's! Always be conscious of being sensitive to Him both with His leading to a person to talk to and the words to say while you're talking.

Find a friend to partner with. There is a special power in the biblical 2 x 2 model.

Remember the practical things:
1. Don't have fowl body odors when talking with others. Use breath mints, deodorant, a tooth brush, and wash your clothes periodically. Don't look "frumpy" unless talking to "frumpy" people.
2. Don't carry your Christian habits into the conversation. Leave your big Bibles at home and only have your Bible App or a Pocket N.T.
3. Don't talk "Christianese". This is weird around unbelievers. Don't speak in tongues, or say things like, "Hallelujah!", "PTL", "the blood of the Lamb", or the "Word of God" (call it the Bible), etc.

4. Be a friend and show respect. Sinners are never a "target". They are a new acquaintance. If they're bored, you thank them and stop. If there is "peace" you stay and build the relationship. This was Jesus' advice from Luke 10

Why A "One Minute" Witness? Two reasons:

1. **Brevity** rules in this age! This is a "sound-byte" age. People all over the world are in a faster mode. We must "become all things to all men so by all possible means we can win them". Besides, you can always make a witness longer if we have the time and they are interested.

2. **Clarity** rules in any age! We need to know where we are going conversationally. Too often our thoughts aren't clear and we ramble on without making the main thing the main thing. The main thing is always your personal story (your witness)

If you're near one of our Seminars, I will guarantee that it will be the best two days you have ever spent. If you are a Pastor, talk with other denominational leaders or heads of Pastor's leagues and see if you can get a minimum of 40 pastors together and we'll fly a team out to your area for a two day seminar that will change your community forever.

Next, make witnessing the "New Normal" of your own lifestyle and that of your Church. Then celebrate with new Believers their new found discovery of Redemption! Open the Sunday Pulpit to "victory reports" from those who had cool witnessing reports from the previous week. If that report giver has a new believer in the church, rejoice with them. Don't put them on the spot. Just rejoice with them.

There is nothing more exciting than fresh new Sinners-saved-by-grace sitting in the church pew, and hanging out with the Family. We read about the *"glad and sincere hearts"* of the people of God as God *"added to the church daily those who should be saved"* in Acts 2.

It's time to bring lots of fresh new "Autograph Candidates" into the church so they can begin their road to their destiny!

Its time for a CELEBRATION!

Chapter Twenty Two

The Finished Painting

The "brushstrokes" of this book are done, but the Brushstrokes of the Creator in your life are just beginning! You will be one of the most valuable works in His collection... Finished with His own Brushstrokes and Autographed by His own Hand! An Autograph of <u>His</u> Autographs is what you are and is what you're becoming! Never to be replicated!

The best the devil can do is to try to hide you, but don't worry. The Holy Spirit has a great interest in you being His ally! And He's not an amateur in giving you surprise venues in which to shine! That's ok! Don't *"hide your light under a bushel"* of false humility. Neither must you hide it under a bushel of pride! Just *"let it shine"!* When done right, it will *"glorify your Father in Heaven"*, and He will use it in His "Autographing" purposes for others!

Some pretty important people said that you should let your light shine:!

      Jesus said, *"Let your light so shine before men..."*

      Paul put it this way, *"We commend ourselves to every man's conscience in the sight of God."* The

Brush Strokes of Jesus in your life will touch everyone's lives as they "know and read" the Living letter that you are!

Daniel the prophet: *"You will shine like the stars!"* Daniel 12:3

Then, when we transition from this earthly life, we will hear, *"well done thou good and faithful servant. Enter thou into the joy of the Lord"*. He will give us the crowns that we will lay before Him in honor. We will meet not only loved ones, but all those that our lives have touched on earth. He will assign us the places that we will rule and reign with him in Heaven depending on how well we yielded to His work in us in this life. His justice will be perfect. No one can take issue with it! All things will be *"naked and open with whom we have to do".* Though our works will be *"tested with fire"*, our foundation of Christ will be guaranteed.

One time, my son and I got lost in the Boundary Waters Canoe Area which is a National Wilderness between Minnesota and Canada. We had gotten confused as we were going down a series of rapids and turned North and ended up lost in some remote Canadian lakes. We knew we were in Canada because we stumbled across a Wilderness Campsite, and it had no "U.S Forest Service" fire grate. We frantically tried to recover ourselves with more hours of paddling and we continued until our butts and arms were too sore to continue.

I said to Brian, "do you think we can find our way back to that Canadian campsite and stay there tonight?" We methodically retraced our path. My 14 year old son did a miraculous job of remembering tree lines, peninsulas and bays and we found the Campsite near dusk. I climbed a hill to see if there was any cell service...none! We were truly at the mercy of the elements. As we set up camp, I told him,

"Let's do everything by the book. Gather firewood and keep it dry for tomorrow, put our food pack in a tree to keep it from animals, and above all, be careful we don't burn ourselves or hurt ourselves.

I assessed our food and found we had very little left because we were on the 7th day of an 8-day wilderness trip. We planned out the rationing of it and sat down with the map to try to figure out what went wrong. Our map only went to the U.S. border so we would have to find our way back to the U.S.

We analyzed the problem and we realized the mistake we had probably made and believed we could recover...if we could just get back to the U.S. side.

The sun greeted us the next morning. "Hey Brian, wake up. Hey, at least it didn't rain. Let's pray and load up and try to find our way out".

I learned in 5th grade Geography that the U.S. is South of Canada and with sun low, we knew which way was south. We picked our way through the lakes; again with Brian's uncanny memory helping us navigate. Suddenly, the map seemed to make some sense. I said, I think the rapids we came down are right over there". Indeed they were. I said, "If we're right, there should be a Campsite with a fire grate right over there". We hurriedly paddled and Brian volunteered to climb the hill and look. All of a sudden, I hear a "Yahoo! Dad, there's a grate!" We were found! We knew where we were. Now our map made sense.

The sky never seemed more blue! As we paddled away, I asked the Lord, "What are you teaching me through this?" He said, "Use it as an illustration for those who have wandered in disobedience from the right path. Tell them they have to first acknowledge they are lost. Then they need to go back to the last point where they knew they were right before they can continue their life's journey"

I use it for that purpose now! Are you confused and maybe lost and are you trying to cover it up by "paddling" more fervently hoping no one will find out? Let me help with a rescue sequence you must follow right now:
1. Acknowledge you're lost. You're confused. You need direction.
2. Find a Haven for prayer, thought, and contemplation. (the Canadian campsite)
3. Start your way back to the time or place that you were not lost. To the place where your "map" was still working.
4. Now, find clear direction with the "map" of God leading your life
5. Rejoice and be thankful to God and...enjoy life again!

Step number 4 is usually accompanied by going back to Christian fellowship, getting back to your Personal Devotions, forgiving, asking forgiveness, or having a change of mind about some things you did wrong. Getting into a trust/accountability relationship with a buddy of the same gender always helps. If God had clearly told you to do something and instead you did like Jonah and "caught a ship to Tarshish" to get away from God...well, you know what you need to do! It's just good you turned around before you got swallowed by a whale!!!...or, maybe you did? Well, even if you did, never forget that Jonah's story was symbolic of the very resurrection of Christ! Even if you got "swallowed by a whale", you can still "cry out to God from the belly of the whale"! Christ will take your hand! God has a Resurrection for you too! Then breathe some better air. Nothing worse than the belly of a whale!

Can't wait to hear more about the Brushstrokes of the Creator in your life!

> ***"It is God who worketh in me to do and to will of His good pleasure" Philippians 2:13***

> *"Come write Your Name in this clay! Come put your name on this picture!"*
>
> -Julie Meyer

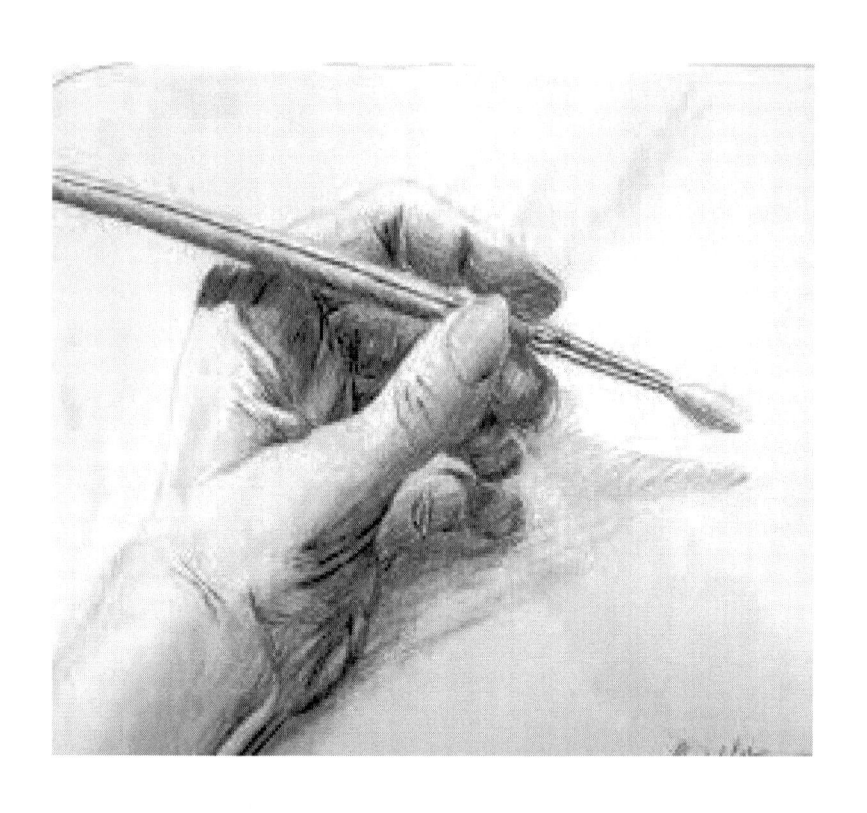

A Chronology of my Autographing

January 1949-Nearly Aborted
June 7, 1949 – Wow, I made it! Thanks mom!
1949-1958 – Formative years with my Dad
June 1954 – Dad discovers his heart valve is damaged and has surgery.
1954-1958 – Dad lives with heart damage and dies having second surgery
1958 – 1961 – Unstable years
1961- 1966 – Abusive years
1966-My stepdad evicts me
1965- 1969 – 1954 Buick years with my Cousin
1966-1979 – I'm Discovered! Plastics Company Years
Feb 3, 1973 – Salvation!
August, 1974 – Call to Full-time ministry
December, 1974 – 1st Date with Ellen
1975-1978 – NCBC
August 7, 1976 Married Ellen
1976-1983 – Youth Ministry, Radio ministry and Koinonia A/G
March 27, 1978 Chris born
February 25, 1980 Tim born
August 19, 1981 Michael born
1983-1989 – YWAM
August 8, 1984 Mandy born
1987-1990 Key Ministries
November 23, 1988 Moved to Glenwood to plant a Spirit-Filled Church and stabilize my kid's education
1991 – Started Dove International
1992-2010- Dove's hot time with Mexico Outreaches. Over 100,000 come to Christ.
November 1994 Brian born
November 2006-present. Evangelist with Oasis in India, Africa, and Latin America. God's promised me 100,000 more souls. I'm getting close!